Carleton Renaissance Plays in Translation

Girolamo Bargagli

THE FEMALE PILGRIM
(La Pellegrina)

Translated, with Introduction and Notes, by

Bruno Ferraro

Dovehouse Editions Canada

1988

Canadian Cataloguing in Publication Data

Bargagli, Girolamo, 1537–1586.
  The Female Pilgrim: La Pellegrina

(Carleton Renaissance plays in translation; 12)
Translation of: La Pellegrina.
Bibliography: p.
ISBN 0-919473-77-6

I. Ferraro, Bruno II. Title. III. Title:
La Pellegrina. IV. Series.

PQ4607.B33P4413 1988 852'.3 C88-090033-4

Printed in Canada

Copyright ©1988, Dovehouse Editions Canada

For information on distribution and for all orders write to:
Dovehouse Editions Canada
32 Glen Ave.
Ottawa, Canada
K1S 2Z7

For information about the series write to:
The Editors, Carleton Renaissance Plays in Translation
c/o the Department of English
Carleton University
Ottawa, Ontario,
K1S 5B6

No part of this book may be translated or reproduced in any form, by print, photoprint, microfilm, microfiche, or any other means, without written permission from the publisher. We would like to be informed of all occasions when this text is used for theatrical performance; please write for permission.

Carleton Renaissance Plays in Translation

General Editors: Donald Beecher, Massimo Ciavolella

Editorial Advisors:
J. Douglas Campbell (Carleton)
Peter Clive (Carleton)
Louise George Clubb (Harvard)
Bruno Damiani (Catholic University of America)
Louise Fothergill-Payne (Calgary)
Peter Fothergill-Payne (Calgary)
Amilcare A. Iannucci (Toronto)
Jean-Marie Maguin (Montpellier)
Domenico Pietropaolo (Toronto)
Anthony Raspa (Chicoutimi)
José Ruano de la Haza (Ottawa)
Pamela Stewart (McGill)

Carleton Renaissance Plays in Translation offers the student, scholar, and general reader a selection of sixteenth-century masterpieces in modern English translation, most of them for the first time. The texts have been chosen for their intrinsic merits and for their importance in the history of the development of the theatre. Each volume contains a critical and interpretive introduction intended to increase the enjoyment and understanding of the text. Reading notes illuminate particular references, allusions, and topical details. The comedies chosen as the first texts have fast-moving plots filled with intrigues. The characters, though cast in the stock patterns of the genre, are witty and amusing portraits reflecting Renaissance social customs and pretensions. Not only are these plays among the most celebrated of their own epoch, but they directly influenced the development of the comic opera and theatre throughout Europe in subsequent centuries.

In print:

Odet de Turnèbe, *Satisfaction All Around (Les Contens)*
Translated with an Introduction and Notes by Donald Beecher

Annibal Caro, *The Scruffy Scoundrels (Gli Straccioni)*
Translated with an Introduction and Notes by Massimo Ciavolella
and Donald Beecher

Giovan Maria Cecchi, *The Owl (L'Assiuolo)*
Translated with an Introduction and Notes by Konrad Eisenbichler

Jean de La Taille, *The Rivals (Les Corrivaus)*
Translated with an Introduction and Notes by H.P. Clive

Alessandro Piccolomini, *Alessandro (L'Alessandro)*
Translated with an Introduction and Notes by Rita Belladonna

Gian Lorenzo Bernini, *The Impressario (Untitled)*
Translated with an Introduction and Notes by Donald Beecher and
Massimo Ciavolella

Jacques Grévin, *Taken by Surprise (Les Esbahis)*
Translated with an Introduction and Notes by Leanore Lieblein and
Russell McGillivray

Lope de Vega, *The Duchess of Amalfi's Steward (El mayordomo de la
duquesa de Amalfi)*
Translated with an Introduction and Notes by Cynthia Rodriguez-Badendyck

Comparative Critical Approaches to Rennaisance Comedy
Edited by Donald Beecher and Massimo Ciavolella

Pietro Aretino, *The Marescalco (Il Marescalco)*
Translated with an Introduction and Notes by Leonard G. Sbrocchi and
J. Douglas Campbell

Lope de Rueda, *The Interludes*
Translated with an Introduction and Notes by Randall W. Listerman

Girolamo Bargagli, *The Female Pilgrim (La Pellegrina)*
Translated with an Introduction and Notes by Bruno Ferraro

In preparation:

Leone de Sommi, *A Comedy of Betrothal (Tsahoth B'dihutha D'kiddushin)*
Translated with an Introduction and Notes by Alfred S. Golding in
consultation with Reuben Ahroni

About the Harrowing of Hell: A Seventeenth-Century Ukrainian Play
Translated with an Introduction and Notes by Irena R. Makaryk

Acknowledgement

I wish to acknowledge my debt to my colleagues Tim Nelson, Department of English (University of New England, Armidale, Australia,) who patiently read the play, revised the English expression and contributed many valuable suggestions, to Laura Riccò, Dipartimento di Italianistica (Università degli Studi di Firenze) for several indispensable clarifications concerning the Italian text and for supplying the photocopies of material unavailable in Australia, to Professors Don Beecher, Massimo Ciavolella and Anthony Raspa for their careful scrutiny of this translation.

We wish to thank the Italian Embassy in Ottawa for their support and encouragement in the publication of this volume.

INTRODUCTION

Life

Though much is known about Girolamo Bargagli's activity within the *Accademia degli Intronati*, his correspondence with a number of eminent personalities of his times and his literary production, little is known of his personal life.[1] Furthermore, the little biographical information at our disposal does not always help in establishing a precise date for his activities and literary compositions. Girolamo Bargagli was born in Siena in 1537, but we have no details regarding the day and month; he was the son of Giulio and Ortensia Urgieri. Girolamo's two brothers, Scipione[2] (1540–1612) and Celso[3] (1543–1593), became famous in their respective fields of specialisation: letters and legal studies. Scipione is remembered for his work on the Sienese language, *Il Turamino*, for his *Trattenimenti* (not dissimilar in style and content from Girolamo's *Dialogo*) and for his collection of devices, *La prima parte delle Imprese* (followed by a second and third part). Celso excelled in the legal profession, holding for ten years the prestigious chair of law at the University of Macerata and then the position of visiting professor in the same discipline at the University of Siena. Scipione and Celso showed an interest not only in Girolamo's literary production but also in his family affairs; Girolamo had married countess Silveria d'Elci on February 22, 1585, and had a son the following February. About March 1586 Girolamo was writing to Celso in Macerata informing him of an ailment which was preventing him from leaving the house. The same illness could have been the cause of his death later in the year. At the time of his death, Silveria was pregnant with the second child, another boy, to be born on April 22, 1587, an event that is mentioned in Scipione's second dedicatory letter in Cerreta's edition of *La Pellegrina*. From Girolamo's testament and a series of letters exchanged between Scipione and Celso, we learn of the part the two brothers played in looking after the widow and her two children, and the background to the presentation of the play to the Grand Duke.[4] At the age of twenty, after an adolescence spent on humanistic studies, Girolamo entered the Academy where he adopted the pseudonym of *Materiale*[5] and participated in the proceedings with a collection of poems, about fifty sonnets and two madrigals. In these poetical compositions Girolamo describes the events that shook his city in those years and expresses his aspiration for peace and social stability. In the area of prose, though his *Dialogo de' Giuochi* was first published in 1572 it was composed as early as 1564, if not in the summer of 1563.[6] In the *Dialogo*, dedicated to Isabella de' Medici Orsini, duchess of Bracciano, Girolamo expresses his regret for the lapse of traditions of the academy—namely the gatherings and the intellectual debates. Besides his display of erudition and his literary preferences, Girolamo manifests (especially in the second part of the *Dialogo*) the influence of the Counter-Reformation, and he reflects, as an author, the caution and care exercised by writers in that period. Girolamo's disappointment and frustration with the state of things, together with the departure of his close friend and mentor Fausto Sozzini—known in the Academy by the pseudonym of *Il Frastagliato*—may have precipitated his decision to abandon literary circles and to immerse himself in legal studies, for which he had already manifested a certain interest as early as 1561. Though we have no document indicating where and when Girolamo completed his legal studies, we know that he first taught at the University of Siena, where he appears with the title of lecturer for the academic year 1563–1564. Subsequently he was called to Florence to take up an appointment as a judge in the Civil Court, only to return to Siena for the academic year 1567–1568 as a professor in legal studies at the local university. It is during this first period of involvement in his legal career that Girolamo is called upon to compose *La Pellegrina*. As we shall see, there is some problem in dating the play, though it is certain that it was written some time between 1564 and 1568. Despite the fact that it was called a comedy, *La Pellegrina* also fitted the prescription for tragicomedy in the terms set out by Giovan Battista Guarini: "it had a 'well woven plot', it was 'stocked with good manners', its wit was used as 'seasoning and not for the main course', and it had an intricate action that plunged its characters into despair and then raised them to happiness."[7] Whilst engaged in the writing of this play—and despite the collaboration of two other *Intronati*, as we shall see later on—Girolamo does not mention this activity in any of his correspondence and, unfortunately, not much is known about

Girolamo for the period he spent in Florence and later in Genoa. He went back to Florence for a six-year period in 1568 and from there to Genoa in 1574 where he was appointed Auditor of the Civil Court and, for a brief period, Chief Magistrate. Though we have no information about his return to Siena, we learn from his correspondence that he was in the city from 1582 to 1586; just before his death Girolamo was to return to Genoa to accept the post of Auditor in the Criminal Court. Girolamo Bargagli died in Siena in October, 1586; he was forty-nine years old.

Girolamo Bargagli, *Materiale Intronato*

At the time when Girolamo Bargagli joined the *Accademia degli Intronati*, the Academy was thirty years old (or thirty-two, being founded in 1525 or 1527) and was undergoing a new lease on life, of cultural and theatrical activity under the drive of Alessandro Piccolomini who was responsible for its reopening after he returned to Siena from his voluntary exile in Rome.[8] Without dwelling on the Academy's activities prior to Girolamo's entry, it must be remembered that the main role of the Academy was that of providing a kind of *salon littéraire* for the discussion of humanistic and literary pursuits. Members of the Academy belonged to the upper social classes and, despite the fact that the Academy's rules prohibited all discussions of matters of state, the members were inevitably drawn to politics. The Sienese intellectuals, until the fall of the city in 1559, had longed to obtain their independence from Florence and from the Empire, and had initially hoped that the Emperor himself, Charles V, would have initiated some reforms of a political and ecclesiastical nature. They were bitterly disappointed when, after the treaty of Cateau-Cambrésis,[9] Siena came under the direct control of Medicean rule. While the theatre of the *Intronati* had in earlier years reflected the Sienese intellectuals' hopes and aspirations,[10] after the late 50's there is a passive acceptance of the *status quo* and the works of the *accademici* reflect, if anything, a pro-Spanish and a pro-Medicean attitude highlighted by numerous encomiastic references. It is against this political and social background that Girolamo entered the Academy around 1557 and produced his brief collection of poems; the Academy, as we know, was temporarily closed during the siege and its reopening was celebrated with the staging of *L'Ortensio* in 1561 in honour of Cosimo I.[11] Despite the excitement caused by Cosimo's visit and his honorary membership in the Academy, the Academy—and the whole city of Siena—lay in a state of torpor and apathy, only worsened by general indifference and an obsessive ecclesiastical censorship. Girolamo's correspondence with his friend Fausto Sozzini, compelled to flee because of his heretical ideas,[12] provides a vivid documentation of the state of things. Sozzini was one of the few *Intronati* of declared anti-Spanish views[13] and a fervent believer in the superiority of humanistic studies over legal ones as he states in a famous letter to Girolamo, dated April 20, 1563.[14]

Though we do not know exactly when the decision to sacrifice literary pursuits in favour of a legal career matured in Girolamo, we can safely say that the *Dialogo* can be seen as a personal and spiritual testimonial, as the epilogue to a period which had been hallmarked by pleasant entertainments and witty orators and as a dream, albeit illusory, for a future revival of the Academy within an independent Siena. In the *Dialogo*—following the model set by Castiglione's *Cortegiano*—Bargagli describes the conversation which took place in 1557–1558 on the occasion of Marcantonio Piccolomini's return to Siena; his work is an important record of the revived activities of the *Intronati* and of their ideology. Bargagli defends the independence of the Academy and advocates its importance as a model of perfect civil life and of social intercourse. In the pursuit of the *piacevoli studi*, the pleasant intellectual studies, Bargagli tries to give, through the metaphor of the *giuoco*[15] (the game or play, indeed play-acting at times), the "idealised" catalogue of games intellectuals (and especially intellectual women) can or cannot play in order to entertain one another, and he provides a sort of suggested 'reading list' for the participants. The nature of *il giuoco* is so well conceptualised in terms of scenic and theatrical presentation that it is not difficult to see how Bargagli was influenced by his participation in the *Intronati*'s collective theatrical activities. We can even isolate a certain nomenclature—*azione, tempo, personaggio*, etc.[16]—which can only point to Bargagli's awareness of the theatre as a medium, and also to the fact that he wouldn't have found it too difficult to devise the plot of a play and to structure it according to the theatrical canons of the times. Since we know that the *Dialogo* was written in 1563 and since the earliest conjectural date for the composition of *La Pellegrina* is 1564 it would appear safe to conclude that the play follows the *Dialogo* and not *vice versa*.[17]

In the organization of the plot and of the characters of *La Pellegrina*, Bargagli shows that he is aware of Piccolomini's *Della Instituzion morale*[18] and of his ideas on the theatre expressed in the letters accompanying the editions of *La Sfera del mondo*;[19] this is specifically evidenced in the discussion between master and servant (Act III, sc. iv). Piccolomini's influence is also to be found in the way Bargagli presents his characters and their behavioural idiosyncrasies. In the tripartite distribution of labour mentioned by Piccolomini in the oft quoted letter to Francesco de' Medici[20] Bargagli is entrusted with the task of devising and controlling the action of *La Pellegrina:* Sozzini is to look after the language (though he is held responsible for the presence of the numerous anti-clerical tirades in the text of the play[21]) and Piccolomini himself is to be the overseer. In this letter Piccolomini refuses the commission, stating that he has already had to decline a similar request from Ferdinando the previous year. This further refusal is in line with Piccolomini's intention to distance himself from the *Intronati*'s team effort; he had also manifested such an intention on the occasion of the production of *L'Ortensio*. Piccolomini's motives in wanting to avoid the commission of a play from the Medici family without prejudicing his ecclesiastical career have been widely discussed by Cerreta[22] and Celse.[23]

With *La Pellegrina* Bargagli, *Materiale Intronato*, seems to develop further on stage material that he had begun in the *Dialogo*; the play provides, through some of its characters, a continuation of the *Dialogo* with its civil conversation among intellectuals. Bargagli writes a comedy of sentiments and manners in which the scenes dealing with love, honour, faith, loyalty and obedience testify to the theatrical taste of the times (as we shall see later on) and to a morality which could exist only in a period of religious and political stability.[24] Bargagli is aware of the ladies' presence in the Academy and, in homage to them, he complies with the tendency of the times: in his play he introduces romantic and sentimental aspects, especially with his female characters, and makes a woman the protagonist of the play; likewise, in the *Dialogo*, women were brought to the fore and urged to participate and debate in matters of interest to them.

History of *La Pellegrina*'s Text

The precise date of *La Pellegrina* remains still undecided despite the efforts, in recent years, of two scholars: N. Borsellino and F. Cerreta. In his article, "The Sienese manuscript of Bargagli's *Pellegrina*,"[25] Cerreta describes the codex H. XI.24, held at the Biblioteca Comunale of Siena, and concludes that the manuscript is in Girolamo's handwriting and bears the corrections of his brother Scipione, who edited the play for the first performance (though we have no way of ascertaining which was the actual text used on that occasion) and for the *princeps* edition in 1589. The codex also contains Scipione's two dedicatory letters (the second of which was to accompany the Bonetti *princeps* edition of 1589); the text of the play, in the version intended by Girolamo, is reproduced by Cerreta in his 1971 critical edition. Cerreta's claim—that the Sienese manuscript in the version corrected by Scipione constitutes the text on which the *princeps* edition is modelled—is a strong and convincing one, and his conclusions hold even after the discovery of yet another autographed manuscript of the play in the Vatican library, the Patetta 357.[26] As for the dating of the play, Cerreta relies on the information contained in two letters: one (undated) written by A. Piccolomini to Francesco de' Medici, which we have already had occasion to mention; another, written on January 18, 1568 (according to Cerreta) by the cardinal Ferdinando de' Medici, in which he thanks Piccolomini and his two collaborators (Bargagli and Sozzini) and acknowledges receipt of the play.[27] The importance of Piccolomini's letter to Francesco lies in the fact that he states that he had to refuse the commission of the play and to enlist the collaboration of his two *Intronati* colleagues;[28] hence Ferdinando's note of thanks to all three of them. From the above documentation, Cerreta concludes first, that since Piccolomini states that he has not written a play or has not been associated with the theatre in twenty-five years (he composed *L'Alessandro* in 1544) Piccolomini's letter should be dated 1568–1569; second, that since Ferdinando's note of thanks is dated January 18, 1567–1568, it can be inferred that Ferdinando's request was made shortly before this date and that *La Pellegrina* was composed no later than 1567–1568; third, that since Scipione mentions in his first dedicatory letter that Girolamo composed the play after his return from Florence, and moreover, that since we know that Girolamo was back in Siena for the academic year 1567–1568, it can be said that the play was composed during this particular Sienese stay.

For his part, Borsellino also partly based his theory on Piccolomini's letter. But he also follows Sanesi's idea that the undated letter by Piccolomini so resembles in content and style another by him to Claudio Saracini written on April 14, 1565,[29] that he believes the undated one must have been written that same year. On this evidence Piccolomini's letter, in which he mentions that in the previous year he had been contacted by Ferdinando, indicates that the play was composed in 1564; of course, had we been in possession of Francesco's original request we could have resolved the dating of Piccolomini's letter.

Borsellino goes on to say that Scipione's statement in his first dedicatory letter—that Girolamo was directly commissioned by Ferdinando (now Grand Duke of Tuscany) to write the play—is to be discarded since Piccolomini's undated letter and Ferdinando's letter of thanks indicate that there had been a tripartite division of labour.[30] Furthermore, Scipione's statement that Girolamo was to write the play after his return to Siena is also to be discarded because Borsellino believes that Girolamo hadn't left for Florence yet and hadn't even been introduced to Ferdinando. Borsellino concludes that Scipione's memory must have betrayed him and that he willingly or unconsciously falsified the truth in order to establish a closer contact between his family and the Medici ruler.[31]

As we can see from the above the same documents lend themselves to two separate dates for the composition of *La Pellegrina*; moreover, despite the discovery of the Patetta 357 manuscript, neither of the two scholars has revised his theories since 1974. Cerreta, in his article on the Vatican manuscript, states that such a manuscript does not impair the importance of the Sienese codex and does not detract from the validity of his theories and of his edition in which he reproduces Girolamo's text without Scipione's mutilations and changes.[32] The problem of the dating of *La Pellegrina* is, however, all too intriguing to be left dormant, especially since no attempt has been made to review Borsellino's and Cerreta's theories vis-à-vis the textual evidence brought out by the Patetta manuscript; I shall try to do so as briefly as possible.

In Act V sc. ii (not sc. i as Patetta suggests) the police officer refers to the ruling prince of the Medici family with the title of *Sua Altezza*, Your Highness, a title which was conferred on Cosimo I by Pope Pius V only in December 1569 but which was used, according to Cerreta, in a *de facto* fashion as early as 1565.[33] Cerreta argues for this reason that the play must have been composed at least after 1565. Patetta points out that in the manuscript discovered by him, *Sua Altezza* was originally *Sua Eccellenza*, Your Excellency, and that this correction is important for the dating of the play. From Patetta's and Cerreta's analysis of the manuscript the following observations can be made. First, if the play had been written long after 1565, i.e. after the title of *Sua Altezza* had been firmly associated with the name of Cosimo I, then it would not have made sense to write *Sua Eccellenza* in the first place. Second, Cerreta is convinced that the Patetta manuscript is in Girolamo's handwriting and that the corrections are to be attributed to either Piccolomini or to Sozzini. Girolamo's original *Eccellenza* can be justified by the fact that Cosimo was referred to with this title as late as 1569 and that the correction to *Altezza* is due to a more scrupulous and reverential zeal on the part of one of his two collaborators. Third, since the correction appears only in the Patetta manuscript and not in the Sienese, it can be argued that the Patetta manuscript represents an earlier version of the Sienese where *Sua Altezza* (without any corrections) appears in Girolamo's handwriting. Cerreta reaches the same conclusion by means of another approach. He analyses the number of scenes and repartees in the Sienese manuscript and surmises that Girolamo adopted some (but not many) of his collaborators' recommendations.[34] That Girolamo did not accept all of his collaborators' suggestions can be verified by comparing the Vatican manuscript with the Sienese one before the latter was expurgated by Scipione.

Though I don't purport to provide any conclusive evidence to the history of the text, I am drawn to venture the following solution which would account for the textual correction of the Patetta manuscript and also for some of the historical conditions set by Piccolomini's letter. At the time he writes the letter, Bargagli is in Florence while Sozzini is still in Siena. This is, therefore, a probable sequence of events: Bargagli is asked to write the play during his first stay in Florence (1565–1567) and submits the text to his two collaborators who reside in Siena when he returns home; in fact, we know that Piccolomini's undated letter was written in Siena and we know that Sozzini was in Siena for a certain period after his return from France (1562–1563) and before he went to Florence for another ten years. The play is commissioned by Ferdinando who at the time is still a cardinal, having been ordained by Pius IV in 1565; for this reason, I presume, Borsellino suggests that the *principe* mentioned in Act I, sc. viii is Ferdinando. I tend to agree with Cerreta and believe that the reference is to the ruling prince, Cosimo I. The text of the play—bearing the corrections and alterations evident in the Patetta manuscript—is returned to Bargagli. One of the corrections is the all important one about Cosimo's title; we can hypothesize that at the time of writing the first draft of the play, such a title had not been widely used but had become accepted *de facto* by the time the two collaborators reviewed the text. The title *Sua Altezza*, in this correction, can only refer to Cosimo because at the time when the play is revised by Sozzini and Piccolomini, Ferdinando is not yet Grand Duke (he will inherit this title in 1587). Since Ferdinando's letter to A. Piccolomini is dated January 18, 1567–1568, and since we can presume that Ferdinando would not thank the writer for something that had taken place long before, it can be deduced that Girolamo composed his play during the end of his Florentine stay (or at the beginning of the academic year 1567–1568), that the play was then reviewed by Piccolomini and Sozzini in Siena during the academic year 1567–1568 and returned to Girolamo who chose to incorporate part of the suggestions and who wrote a 'fair' copy with *Sua Altezza* in its proper place. This version, the Sienese codex of the Biblioteca Comunale, was then presented to Ferdinando who handed it back to Girolamo as we can infer from Scipione's correspondence. The sequence of events I have suggested reconciles most of the divergences between Borsellino's and Cerreta's theories. Though it does not provide a more precise date for the actual composition, it does justify some of the discrepancies noted, including those contained in Scipione's first dedicatory letter,[35] as already pointed out by Borsellino. If we want to follow the history of the text to its final stages, we have to turn to Scipione who, upon a generic request for a play from one of the Grand Duke's magistrates, Signor Baili Augustini, sends to Ferdinando the text of *La Pellegrina* as it is in the Sienese manuscript, since so far no evidence has been found of a *codex interpositus*. From a reading of Scipione's letter[36] to the Grand Duke on February 23, 1587–1588, we can see that Scipione is hoping that Ferdinando will use the play for the 1589 wedding celebrations. In order to ingratiate himself with the newly-elected Grand Duke, Scipione sends the play with an accompanying letter dated March 4, 1587–1588; this is Scipione's first dedicatory letter. At this point we must conjecture again that the play was returned to Scipione with a request for expurgation. By now Girolamo and Piccolomini are dead, Sozzini has been abroad since 1575 and Scipione seems the logical choice for such a revision.

As for the reason for such a revision, Borsellino argues that the play couldn't have been performed in its original version because of the anticlerical tirades.[37] Cerreta points out that the *Intronati* playwrights interspersed their plays with harsh denunciations of the clergy and that by the late sixteenth century such broadsides had become conventions on the Italian stage and would not have constituted any polemical dissent:

What is certain, however, is that the detection and excision of the passages in question were due to a more rigorous application of the Roman Curia's decrees regulating the press. . . . It was only after 1564 that a concerted effort was made to expunge from books injurious references to the clergy like those of the Sienese manuscript.[38]

This could well justify the fact that the Sienese manuscript bears the signature of two different officials who cleared the material prior to publication;[39] they did allow, however, some very scathing remarks about priests, especially rich priests as is the case in Act II, sc. v where we can see that the censors and Scipione (who presumably had to follow their directions) cannot find a way out by correcting a word here and there or by substituting some *risqué* expressions as they had done with other passages. Therefore, they eliminate the whole passage which, as a consequence, will not appear in the *princeps* or in subsequent editions. Borsellino also states that it was the Medici's prudence, rather than ecclesiastic censorship, that caused the change of the female protagonist's place of origin from Valencia in Spain to Lyon in France in the *princeps* edition; furthermore, Borsellino states that there is a shift of satire from anti-Spanish to anti-French.[40] Certainly there are no tirades against either country in the text of the play and the change of nationality could be ascribed, according to Cerreta,[41] to two factors: first to honour the country of origin of Ferdinando's bride, Cristina of Lorraine and second, to emphasise the political *rapprochement* made by Ferdinando to France, to signal his disengagement from Spain and to signal a break with the policy pursued by both Cosimo and Francesco.

The text of *La Pellegrina* was subject to a certain amount of travesty and, given the nature of changes alluded to, the selection of the play for performance at the royal wedding of 1589 must have caused Scipione a degree of apprehension. He appears to acknowledge as much in his second dedicatory letter where he parallels the vicissitudes of the play to that of Ferdinando's proposed wedding which had been delayed for a number of reasons. The history of the text of *La Pellegrina* is very interestingly connected to a particularly sensitive moment of Tuscan history and until new light is shed upon the involvement and the movements of Fausto Sozzini in those years, upon the activities and the correspondence of Girolamo Bargagli (especially in those years in which he devoted himself to the *Dialogo* and to *La Pellegrina*), we shall have to rely on a reconstruction of events which, at times, can only be the product of deduction and inferences.

The Plots

One of the striking features of *La Pellegrina* is the absence of a prologue. This absence is all the more significant since the play was performed on such a public and festive occasion as the wedding of the Grand Duke Ferdinando I de' Medici with Cristina of Lorraine.

Sixteenth-century Italian plays were usually introduced by a prologue and, sometimes, we have more than one prologue for the same play; the reason for this is that a different prologue was sometimes written for the specific occasion on which the play was performed. It is extraordinary, therefore, that no prologue was written for *La Pellegrina* for the 1589 performance or for any subsequent performance of the play. The performance of a series of six *intermezzi* might have made it too difficult, from an organizational point of view, to introduce a prologue as well. Despite any conjecture on our part, the fact remains that we have no record of a prologue written by Girolamo Bargagli or by any other person.

The prologue, among other things, was used in sixteenth century Italian plays to summarise the background to the story; in its absence we have to look at the opening scene of *La Pellegrina* for the introduction of the first main plot. Lepida, daughter of Cassandro, has been betrothed to Lucrezio but neither she nor he desires the match. Lepida is secretly in love with the family tutor, Terenzio, who in the end turns out to be a German nobleman in disguise. Lepida, in collusion with her lover, whose child she is bearing, feigns madness in order to thwart her father's plans. Lucrezio is reticent to marry a mad woman; moreover, he doesn't wish to marry: he is convinced to do so by his family only because his former love, Drusilla, has been reported dead. This report proves to be false: Drusilla is alive and has come to Pisa, where the action takes place, to find out what has become of Lucrezio; she is dressed as a pilgrim and escorted by her faithful companion Ricciardo. The action is complicated by the intervention of another suitor, Federigo, who, in his desire to seduce Lepida, discovers her love affair with the family tutor. After various mishaps and misunderstandings the play comes to its *dénouement*: Lepida marries Terenzio who turns out to be Federigo's long lost brother Lucrezio (hence the confusion of names); Lucrezio is reunited with Drusilla who reveals herself to him in the very last scene of the play. In *La Pellegrina* Bargagli reflects to the letter the two levels of structure typical of the *Intronati*'s theatrical production: on one level we find the intrigue and drama of the lovers, and on a second level we have the spectacle of the servants or of minor characters who delay the main action with their rowdiness and comic gags. At first there seems to be no sharp dividing line between the *Intronati*'s plays and normal learned comedy as it is known in sixteenth century Italian theatre, but on closer scrutiny it becomes clear that the Italian theatrical production in the second half of the century (particularly in Siena) is characterised by the presence of more romantic and pathetic elements, with serious and almost tragic implications. From a comedy of intrigue where the *beffa* or trickery held a prominent position, the emphasis is now placed on sentiments and events which bring anguish, suffering and threats of death; all, however, is resolved in a happy outcome and tragedy is hence avoided. This type of comedy, distinct from tragedy or tragicomedy, can be aptly called serious comedy and will eventually lead to the *Commedia dell'Arte* and to other theatrical *genres*: melodrama, tragicomic plays of the Baroque period and the *comédie larmoyante (teatro lacrimoso)* of the mid-eighteenth century.

In serious comedy love is the mechanism which makes characters take on disguises and travel to far away places to seek out their lovers; it is love which creates a series of misunderstandings and cases of mistaken identity. The characters involved in such situations usually discourse on their fate and suffering, on the uniqueness and nobility of their love and on their impeccable code of honour. In *La Pellegrina* the two main plots dealing with the themes outlined above are entrusted to the two pairs of lovers: Drusilla/Lucrezio and Lepida/Terenzio. At a different level Bargagli creates a series of sub-plots (or sheer comic *divertissements*) in which the ridiculous, the slapstick and the rowdy elements are predominant; these scenes slow down the rhythm of the main plots and afford moments of sheer laughter and hedonistic enjoyment. These sketches are aimed at delighting especially the less intellectual members of the audience who would relish situations such as the exchanges between Carletto and Cavicchia when they philolosophize about their social status (Act III, sc. iv),[42] the conversation between Giglietta and Violante about their choice of lovers (Act III, sc. vii), Targhetta's recount to Federigo of his visit to the monastery (Act II, sc. v) and Targhetta's clash with Violante (Act III, sc. iii). As can be seen, most of the scenes in which servants and characters drawn from the populace perform are to be found in Act III; according to the canons of serious comedy Act IV should bring the heroine and hero to the lowest depth of misery and to the highest level of drama. These circumstances are, in turn, reversed in the final act by the customary agnition (recognition of a character thought to be dead or lost for ever) and by the happy ending. Apart from a brief scene between Carletto and Cavicchia in which the two servants exchange pleasanteries about food and wine (Act V, sc. iii), the action of the servants is relegated to the earlier acts. Unlike learned comedy (especially Florentine) in which much of the action revolves around a central *beffa*, in serious comedy there is no major trickery (Lepida's feigned sickness can be considered only a half-hearted trick and not a central device) hence the minor characters never rise to the status of *mattatori*, inventors of machinations or intelligent solutions which have great bearing on the play. It is the lovers who exercise control over the action of the play since they, and not the servants, devise their own ruses.

The Characters

As there is a distinction between the main plots and the sub-plots, so there is a differentiation between the 'high' and the 'low' characters of the play—a differentiation which will be marked by the variation of linguistic registers. Messer Terenzio is a particularly complex figure. He represents the pedant, a traditional figure of derision and laughter in sixteenth-century Italian comedy, who often quotes Latin words (Act I, sc. viii) and uses a language dear to the *accademici* and so reminiscent of Francesco Colonna's *Hypnerotomachia Poliphili*.[43] Bargagli's parody of the pedant in this play could also be seen as the author's caricature of intellectuals in general and, since he is an intellectual himself, as a sort of self-caricature.[44] But Messer Terenzio is also one of the lovers and, in this dual role of lover and pedant, he raises the interesting problem of identity when he analyses his unfortunate state of affairs in Act I, sc. iii. Lucrezio, in all respects, is a rather dull figure and personifies, in a Decameronian fashion, the bourgeois merchant; his interest in money and his views on the proposed marriage with Lepida as a business transaction give rise to some tirades on the part of Carletto (Act I, sc. iv) and of Cassandro (Act I, sc. v and Act IV, sc. i) which highlight what can be termed the 'love-cash nexus' theme of *La Pellegrina*[45] where the actions of a character are motivated by monetary and materialistic considerations rather than by genuine and spontaneous affection. The difference between the two pairs of lovers is also indicated by the degree of sexual freedom enjoyed by them: Lepida is already four months pregnant with Messer Terenzio's child, but Lucrezio has not been able to enjoy Drusilla's amorous favours even after the secret wedding (Act I, sc. iv and Act II, sc. i).

The stark differentiation between the two sets of female characters, Drusilla and Lepida on one side, and a number of female servants drawn from the populace on the other, is in line with the practice of the times to combine the description of lofty and magnanimous behaviour with misogynistic tirades and hedonistic situations. In Drusilla/Lepida we find the embodiment of the code of ethics which was advocated by the Sienese intellectuals—honesty, loyalty and fidelity—and in the couple Violante/Giglietta we recognise the more earthy and scurrilous depiction of woman's behaviour. Such a contrast is also accompanied by a series of comments on women—reminiscent of Piccolomini's *La Raffaella*[46] —in which Bargagli allows (albeit towards the women drawn from the populace) certain uncomplimentary tirades. Again it is in Act III that we find the scene between Cavicchia and Messer Federigo (sc. vi), preceded by a similar dialogue between the German scholar and Targhetta (sc. v) and by another between Giglietta and Violante (sc. ii but also sc. vii) in which the servants manifest openly their ideas on sexuality and on relationships between men and women; these scenes effectively highlight the contrasting behaviour of the 'high' and 'low' characters.

Among the minor characters, Violante also fulfills the role of procuress and bawd, interestingly enough under the guise of the owner of a boarding house; Giglietta is more akin to the traditional maid of sixteenth-century Italian theatre who endeavours to please the young lovers at the expense of the old master. Giglietta is also used at different times to offer unceremonious comments about the medical profession (Act I, sc. i) and the misbehaviour of priests (Act I, sc. ii). She is the only witness to the secret marriage between Lepida and Messer Terenzio during which the two exchange the ring as a symbol of their private wedding (Act I, sc. ii); in an analogous fashion the leitmotif of the ring appears in the projected marriage between Lucrezio and Lepida. The fact that he has not yet given the girl the ring provides the young man with a possible excuse to break off the engagement (Act I, sc. vi). It was quite acceptable in those days for a marriage to be contracted between two parties either in secret or before a witness (usually a servant) as long as a ring was exchanged between the two parties; hence Cassandro's preoccupation (Act I, sc. v), the pilgrim's legalistic enquiry (Act II, sc. vii) and Lucrezio's apparent bigamy since he is secretly married to Drusilla and engaged to Lepida.[47]

Though it is the character of Giglietta who instigates and takes up again in the course of the play (Act I, sc. vi) the anti-ecclesiastical tirades, it is Targhetta who, in a way which is reminiscent of Boccaccio's tirades against priests in the *Decameron* (III, 7), is given the task of delivering the harshest invectives against priests and in particular against those who pamper themselves (Act II, sc. v). It is in this scene, as already stated, that Borsellino sees the main reasons for the expurgation of the manuscript before the 1589 performance. Targhetta, all told, is depicted almost as the traditional Latin parasite who accompanies the *miles gloriosus* and is usually worried about filling his stomach; Targhetta is certainly preoccupied with food (Act II, sc. ii; Act ii, sc. iv and v) but he is also the mouthpiece for a number of quips against the Germans—traditionally known in sixteenth-century Italian comedy for their drinking and lack of taste in food and women (Act II, sc. v).

Messer Federigo seems to provide many characters with the chance of delivering their own thoughts about a range of situations and fits the stereotype image of the foreigner (usually Spanish) who is the butt of jokes and *beffe*. The ridicule reserved for the Spanish characters in the *Intronati*'s later plays is usually devoid of any political connotation and is part and parcel of the traditional comic fashion in which the *miles gloriosus*[48] is treated. There is no difference, therefore, between the Spanish Francisco (*L'Amor Costante*) and the Pisan Malagigi (*L'Alessandro*). Even the *beffa* played on the Spanish soldier Giglio (*Gl'Ingannati*, Act IV, sc. vi)—very similar to that played by Violante on Targhetta (Act III, sc. iii)—is emptied of any political or polemical content. The 'education' of the German scholar is also Cavicchia's preoccupation (Act III, sc. i) when he philosophizes on the quality of love that can be dispensed by women of different social extraction. As a servant, Cavicchia fits his traditional role only in the scene with Violante (Act III, sc. ix) where he shows interest in money and sex and displays a sly manner for obtaining both.

The male companion at the pilgrim's service, Ricciardo, is in tune with the status of his mistress; he speaks and acts more civilly than the other 'low' characters. The whole scene in which Ricciardo, Lucrezio and the pilgrim come face to face (Act II, sc. vi) is an apology to good manners and civil intercourse. Cassandro, as we have seen in his discussions with Lucrezio, displays a merchant's mentality, though he is genuinely interested in his daughter's health and social well-being. Cassandro is not, therefore, a stereotype for the old man of Renaissance comedy: miserly and lecherous. He will rise to the occasion by forgiving Messer Terenzio, by allowing him to be freed to marry Lepida. As with the minor character of Fabrizio in Piccolomini's *L'Alessandro* (Act IV, sc. iii; Act V, sc. v), in *La Pellegrina* it is the minor characters who introduce the encomiastic comments about the Medici family: Ricciardo (Act II, sc. ii) when he praises the ruler for the improved conditions of Pisa (the inference being that Siena will also improve under the Medici rule), Messer Federigo (Act I, sc. viii), the police officer (Act V, sc. ii) and Cassandro (Act IV, sc. vi) when they discuss the Grand Duke's strict laws. More interestingly it is Cassandro who delivers a satirical tirade against the legal profession (Act III, sc. viii), the very career that Bargagli had just decided to follow!

The Language

The language of *La Pellegrina* is literary Tuscan which took on a more pronounced veneer of Sienese when Scipione Bargagli revised the text.[49] From the theatrical point of view the language registers reflect the class distinctions of the characters and are regulated so as to highlight the lofty topics of discussion; in a way which is reminiscent of the main themes of the *Decameron*, we often encounter words, such as *Amore* and *Fortuna*, which are spelt with capital letters. The language of Drusilla, even when she talks with her male companion Ricciardo (Act II, sc. i) is always civil and refined; her language is down to earth and practical only when she advises Cassandro of a remedy for his daughter (Act III, sc. x) and indicts the medical profession (Act IV, sc. ii). Lepida, Messer Terenzio and even Lucrezio display a dual register: they cultivate their syle and syntax when they are talking about love and honour (respectively in Act II, sc. ii; Act I, sc. iii; Act II, sc. vii) while on other occasions they can be abrupt, materialistic and uninspired (respectively in Act II, sc. vi; Act V, sc. iv; Act IV, sc. iii where Lucrezio, exasperated, loses control over his language and addresses Cassandro with the colloquial form: *Lasciami andare*, let me go). Cassandro is always down to earth and does not avoid distributing insults to Giglietta (Act II, sc. vi); the racy effects of the Tuscan and the *double entendres*, puns and sexual innuendos are all left to the servants (Cavicchia in Act II, sc. vii, Violante in Act III, sc. ix, Carletto in Act II, sc. iii).

The scenes with the servants and their racy language make up a fair proportion of the play but, as already stated, these scenes are of secondary importance. It follows that Bargagli strives to show his linguistic expertise in designing and executing in a very precise and cultivated manner the numerous dialogues and repartees uttered by the two pairs of lovers. It is Lucrezio and Drusilla, rather than the servants who dominate the end of the play, and who mastermind the conditions that lead to a successful conclusion to the pilgrimage. It is Drusilla, and not a servant, who delivers the *licenza*; this was a formula of farewell (*valete et plaudite*), addressed to the audience, with which sixteenth-century Italian plays usually ended. It seems that Bargagli, with this last technical expedient, wants to focus the audience's attention, until the very last minute, on his sensitive and eloquent heroine.

Note on the Translation

I have used the text edited by Cerreta, an excellent edition that contains a very good introduction, linguistic annotations and a glossary, the variants of the *princeps* edition, as well as the text edited by Borsellino who bases his edition on the 1605 and 1606 reprints. I have tried to render the original into a contemporary idiomatic English; certain sentences in the original text, especially the dedicatory letters, are complex and pretentious. I have tried to reflect these qualities while avoiding, however, merely *verbatim* renderings and unnecessary repetitions. I have introduced stage directions (indicated by square brackets and italics) to heighten the theatrical 'legibility' of the text; the only two existing stage directions have been kept and indicated by round brackets. I have also maintained throughout the text all the original punctuation marks used by Cerreta in his edition; I have eliminated the dash inserted after a colon before a reported speech.

Sources and Affinities

According to Stiefel and Cerreta it is quite clear that the character of Messer Terenzio, who has to put on a disguise in order to be close to his beloved, is derived from Ariosto's *I Suppositi* and Piccolomini's *Amor Costante*; likewise it is accepted that the discovery and capture of Messer Terenzio in Lepida's room is recurrent in a number of plays: the Intronati's *Gl'Ingannati*, Piccolomini's *Amor Costante*, Grazzini's *I Parentadi*, Bibbiena's *La Calandria*, etc. Lepida's secret marriage to Messer Terenzio has affinities with the story of Galeotto Malatesti in the *Pecorone* (VII, 2) while the motif of the feigned madness is inspired by Grazzini's *La Spiritata*[50] and—according to Mango[51] —by one of Masuccio Salernitano's stories (I, 9) in the *Novellino*. Stiefel and Cerreta abandon the task of searching for a play or plays which might have inspired the title and the character of the female pilgrim because the sources are numerous and it is impossible to ascertain the direct derivation from one particular source or another; in this process also G.M. Cecchi's *Le Pellegrine* is discarded as a direct source of inspiration because, according to Cerreta, the play was only published posthumously in 1855 and deals with a number of female pilgrims rather than just one.[52] Though not published until 1855, *Le Pellegrine* was performed during the 1567 carnival in Florence; after the death of Cosimo I, to whom the play was dedicated in a letter dated January 1, 1566, Cecchi demands that the play be returned to him so that he may change the prologue and add the *intermedi*.[53] Upon closer scrutiny we find the following elements which are common to both plays: the disguise of the young French girl dressed as a boy, and of the fake doctor, Maestro Sinolfo; the pilgrimage of Cangenova from Siena; Fiammetta's feigned sickness; the melodramatic and passionate language used by the lovers (Act II, sc. iii); the misogynistic tirades made by the servants (Act I, sc. i) and by doctor Alberto (Act IV, sc. vi). Though there is no definite evidence of this, it can be claimed that Bargagli, prior to his return to Siena later in that same year, could have very well been present at the 1567 carnival performance of Cecchi's *Le Pellegrine*.

In his search for analogies between the main plot—the relationship between Drusilla and Lucrezio—of *La Pellegrina* and other works, Cerreta claims that there is a similarity with the eleventh story of Sabadino degli Arienti's *Le Porretane*; as for the motif of the apparent death of the protagonist and of the usage of the trinket to establish the identity of the long lost person, Cerreta draws parallels with Boccaccio's story of Messer Torello (*Decameron*, X, 9).[54] Though further erudite research has been conducted by Cerreta into the Scottish ballads and Nicolò Bonaparte's *La Vedova*,[55] it can be concluded that, given the popularity of the theme of the pilgrimage and of some of the other *leit-motifs* which make up the plot of the play, it is impossible to establish the exact sources for the derivation of Bargagli's *La Pellegrina*. One can be more safe in accepting the suggestion that the name Drusilla derives from the *Orlando Furioso* (Canto XXVI) as do other names and characters of the play; Ariosto's masterpiece was, after all, the main source of reference for the *Intronati* and for the participants in the *Dialogo*.

With regard to *La Pellegrina* as a model for later Italian or French plays, Cerreta suggests that the play's diffusion at the end of the sixteenth century was impeded by a change in public taste and by the advent of the *Commedia dell'Arte*.[56] However, it can be argued that the theme of *La Pellegrina* very well presented a *leit-motif* for some *canovacci*—such as those of *La Forestiera* included in Basilio Locatelli's repertoire[57] —which were regularly performed around the country. Baratto suggests that the theme of the pilgrimage and the subesequent disguise, as depicted in Bargagli's play, will recur frequently in the Italian theatre of later eras; Drusilla could be the forerunner of the protagonist of two of Goldoni's plays: Beatrice (*Il servitore di due padroni*) and Placida (*La bottega del caffè*).[58] It is through the *canovacci* that the theme of *La Pellegrina* could have been discovered by Rotrou whose *La Pélerine Amoureuse, tragicomédie* was first performed in 1634 and then published two years later.[59] Two nineteenth century scholars, J. Vianey[60] and A.L. Stiefel,[61] have studied the interrelation between the French play and Bargagli's, arriving at the conclusion that Rotrou's derivation took place through the mediation of a number of Italian plays which had in turn been derived from the *La Pellegrina*[62] or as a product of *contaminatio* with a number of *scenari* performed in those days in France by Italian actors. This could also account for traces of *La Pellegrina* in Moliere's *Les Femmes savantes*, Regnard's *Les Folies Amoureuses* and Destouche's *La Fausse Agnes*.[63]

Performances of *La Pellegrina*

After Belisario Bulgarini's unsuccessful attempt to stage the play in 1582,[64] the play was finally performed in the course of the festivities[65] for the wedding between Ferdinando de' Medici and Cristina of Lorraine on May 2, 1589.[66] On May 6 the *intermedi* prepared for *La Pellegrina* were used for the performance of *La Zingara* and on May 13 for the performance of *La Pazzia*; on May 15 *La Pellegrina* was performed once more for the benefit of the Venetian ambassadors who had arrived late. The technical expertise of Bernardo Buontalenti, the particular care with which Emilio de' Cavalieri—in collaboration with famous *cameratisti* such as Malvezzi, Marenzio, Caccini, etc.—composed the music, the spectacular production of the *intermedi*, the curiosity of visiting the newly established Medici theatre were all factors which contributed to make the play the *clou* of the fortnight-long festivities. The lengthy accounts which Bastiano de' Rossi[67] gave of the play (published in the same year) and Cristoforo Malvezzi gave of the *intermedi* and of the music (published two years later)[68] testify to the success of the play; it is, therefore, all the more astonishing to ascertain that there is no record of later performances of *La Pellegrina*.[69]

Editions of *La Pellegrina*[70]

Place and Date		Publisher
Siena,	1589	Luca Bonetti (*Editio Princeps*)
Siena,	1589?	Attributed to Matteo Florimi[71]
Siena,	1605	Matteo Florimi who follows the *princeps*
Venice,	1606	Roberto Meglietti who follows the *princeps*
Venice,	1606?	Attributed to Giambattista Pulciani[72]
Siena,	1611	Matteo Florimi who follows his 1605 edition[73]
Siena,	1618	Ibidem
Milan,	1962	G. Feltrinelli (edited by N. Borsellino)
Siena,	1971	Leo. S. Olschki (edited by F. Cerreta)

NOTES TO THE INTRODUCTION

1 Information on G. Bargagli's life and works is to be found in the following: N. Borsellino, *Dizionario biografico degli italiani* (Rome, 1964), vol. VI, 341–343 and *Le Commedie del Cinquecento* (Milan, 1962), vol. I, 429; F. Cerreta, *La Pellegrina* (Florence, 1971), 9–11; G. Bargagli, *Dialogo de' Giuochi*, ed. P. D'Incalci Ermini with Introduction by R. Bruscagli (Siena, 1982), 40.
2 Information on S. Bargagli's life and works is to be found in the following: S. Bargagli, *Il Turamino*, ed. L. Serianni (Rome, 1976), XXVIII–XXXVI; N. Borsellino, *Dizionario biografico degli italiani* cit., 343–346; A. Merenduzzo, "Notizie intorno a Scipione Bargagli," *Bullettino Senese di Storia Patria*, VII, 2 (1900), 326–347; G.M. Mazzucchelli, *Gli scrittori d'Italia* (Brescia, 1763), III, 351; L. Riccò, "Un inedito di Scipione Bargagli," *Filologia Critica*, Anno VIII, fasc. I (1983), 39–107; L. De Angelis, *Biografia degli scrittori senesi* (Siena, 1824), vol. I, 67 and *Memorie del cavalier Girolamo Bargagli e Antonio Malavolti* (Siena, 1828).
3 N. Borsellino, *Dizionario biografico degli italiani* cit., 341; G. Prunai, "Lo studio senese nel primo quarantennio del principato mediceo," *BSSP*, LXVI (1959), 140, 143.
4 L. Riccò, "Vent'anni dopo: Un progetto di riedizione del *Dialogo de' Giuochi*," *Studi di filologia critica offerti dagli allievi a Lanfranco Caretti* (Rome, 1985), vol. I, 261, note 12.
5 L. Sbaragli, "I Tabelloni degli Intronati," *BSSP*, XLIX, fasc. III (1942), 177–197; Girolamo's name appears on the list on p. 193.
6 G. Bargagli, *Dialogo*, ed. cit., 48, note 16.
7 M.T. Herrick, *Italian comedy in the Renaissance* (Urbana, 1960), 179. In her article, "The politics of spectacle: *La Pellegrina* and the *Intermezzi* of 1589," *MLN* (1986), 95–113, K. Newman suggests that "both the character and the plot [of the *Pellegrina*] comform to the conventions of the so-called *commedia grave* or serious comedy characteristic of the late *Cinquecento*." On the subject see L.G. Clubb, "Italian Comedy and the *Comedy of Errors*," *Comparative Literature*, 19 (1967), 240–251 and "Woman as wonder: generic figure in Italian Renaissance and Shakespearean Comedy," *Studies in the Continental background of Renaissance literature* (Durham, 1977), 109–132; J.W. Lever, *Measure for measure* (London, 1965), introduction; A. Kirsch, *Jacobean Dramatic Perspectives* (Charlottesville, 1972). The Italian scholar Cesare Molinari prefers the term 'romantic' to describe the various extraordinary and wonderful events of such a play ("Strutture drammaturgiche e sceniche del teatro cinquecentesco," in *Scene e figure del teatro italiano* 1981, 31) while G. Davico Bonino is interested in underlining the religious-historical impact of *La Pellegrina* in *Il teatro italiano* (Turin, 1977, vol. II, xlv–xlvi).
8 On the history of the Academy and on Sienese culture in the sixteenth cen-

tury see the following: I. Ugurgieri–Azzolini, *Le pompe sanesi* (Pistoia, 1649); E. Cleder, *Notice sur l'Acadèmie italienne des Intronati* (Bruxelles, 1864); L. Petracchi-Costantini, *L'Accademia degli Intronati di Siena e una sua commedia* (Siena, 1928); M. Maylander, *Storia delle Accademie d'Italia* (Bologna, 1929), vol. III, 360 ff.; F. Iacometti, *L'Accademia degli Intronati* (Siena, 1950). On the role of the Academy and Alessandro Piccolomini in particular, see: A. Piccolomini, *L'Alessandro*, ed. F. Cerreta (Siena, 1966), introduction; F. Cerreta, *Alessandro Piccolomini, letterato e filosofo senese nel Cinquecento* (Siena, 1960); D. Seragnoli, "Il progetto drammaturgico di Alessandro Piccolomini: il personaggio e la fabula," in *Il teatro a Siena nel Cinquecento* (Siena, 1980), 93–134; A. Piccolomini, *Alessandro*, trans. R. Belladonna (Ottawa, 1984), introduction; R. Scrivano, "Alessandro Piccolomini," in *Cultura e letteratura del Cinquecento* (Rome, 1966), 11–50; M. Celse, "Alessandro Piccolomini, l'homme du ralliement," in *Les écrivains et le pouvoir en Italie à l'époque de la Renaissance*, ed. A. Rochon (Paris, 1973), première partie), 7–76.

9 For the events concerning the Sienese war, it suffices to refer to the following: A. D'Addario, *Il problema senese nella storia italiana della prima metà del Cinquecento* (Florence, 1958); R. Cantagalli, *La guerra di Siena (1552–1559)* (Siena, 1962).

10 For the political and politicised aspect of the *Intronati*'s theatre see the following: N. Borsellino, "Drammaturgia e società a Siena" in *Rozzi e Intronati* (Rome, 1974), 89–106; A. Mauriello, "Cultura e società nella Siena del Cinquecento," *Filologia Critica*, XVII, fasc. I (1971), 26–48; M. Celse, "Un problème de structure théâtrale: 'beffa' et comédie dans le théâtre des Intronati a Sienne," *Revue des études italiennes*, 15 (1969); N. Newbigin, "Politics and comedy in the early years of the *Accademia degli Intronati* of Siena," in *Il teatro italiano del Rinascimento* (Milan, 1980), 123–134. I take this opportunity to thank Nerida Newbigin (Department of Italian, University of Sydney) for having made available to me research material on the *Intronati*.

11 F. Cerreta, "Clarifications concerning the real authorship of the Renaissance comedy *Ortensio*," *Renaissance News*, X (1957), vol. 2, 63–69; for an opposite view on the authorship of the play *L'Ortensio*, see A.L. Stiefel, "Die Nachahmung italienischer Dramen bei einigen Vorläufern Molières," *Zeitschrift für Französische Sprache und Litteratur*, vol. XXVII, 1904, 189–233.

12 G. Bargagli's involvement with Fausto Sozzini has been somewhat neglected except for the following: V. Marchetti, "Notizie sulla giovinezza di Fausto Sozzini da un copialettere di Girolamo Bargagli," *Bibliothèque d'Humanisme et Renaissance*, vol. XXI (1969), 67–91; by the same author see the following: "Sull'origine e la dispersione del gruppo ereti-

cale dei Sozzini a Siena (1557–1560)," *Rivista storica italiana*, LXXXI (1969), 133–173 and "Antonio Mazzi (1884–1947), uno sconosciuto biografo di Fausto Sozzini," *BSSP*, LXXIII–LXXV (1966–1968), 119–130; D. Cantimori, *Eretici italiani nel Cinquecento* (Florence, 1939); C. Dionisotti, "Chierici e laici," in *Geografia e storia della letteratura italiana* (Turin, 1967), 55–68; G. Pioli, *Fausto Socino, vita-opere-fortuna* (Modena, 1952).
13 A. Mauriello, "Cultura e società nella Siena del Cinquecento" cit., 33.
14 V. Marchetti, "Notizie sulla giovinezza . . . " cit., 89; the letter was first published in a work which also holds interesting information on the heretical circles in sixteenth-century Italy: C. Cantù, *Gli eretici d'Italia* (Turin, 1866), vol. II, 491–496; an analysis of the letter is made by D. Cantimori, *Eretici Italiani* cit., 347–349.
15 In addition to the works already listed, see the following: V. Marchetti, "Il gioco nella formazione culturale di Fausto Sozzini," in *Le regole del gioco e l'eresia* (Bologna, 1981), 7–50; A. Marenduzzo, *Veglie e trattenimenti nella seconda metà del secolo XVI* (Trani, 1901), 1–96; D. Seragnoli, "*Il Dialogo de' Giuochi* di Girolamo Bargagli," in *Il teatro a Siena nel Cinquecento* cit., 181–197.
16 *Dialogo*, ed. cit., part I, 323 ff.; part II, 105 ff.; part II, 439 ff. For the relationship between *gioco* and *teatro* see D. Seragnoli, "Il Dialogo . . . " cit., 186–197.
17 N. Borsellino, "Il manoscritto della *Pellegrina*," in *Rozzi e Intronati* cit., 113.
18 A. Piccolomini, *Della Instituzion morale. Libri XII* (Venice, 1569); see in particular the last two *Libri* and the chapter on the behaviour and the theatrical role of the old characters on stage (p. 317).
19 A. Piccolomini, *La sfera del mondo [. . .] ripolita, accresciuta e fino a sei libri di quattro che erano ampliata e quasi per ogni parte rinnovata e riformata* (Venice, 1573); see in particular the dedicatory letters to Antonio Cocco (dated November 10, 1560 and June 8, 1564) in which Piccolomini speaks of his previous plays and of his plan to write such a treatise on the composition and the structure of plays.
20 The letter, undated, has been published by I. Sanesi, "Per una lettera di Alessandro Piccolomini," in *Studi letterari e linguistici dedicati a Pio Rajna* (Florence, 1911), 757 ff. Sanesi's dating of this letter, 1565, has led Borsellino to believe that *La Pellegrina* was composed in 1564.
21 N. Borsellino, "Il manoscritto della Pellegrina" cit., 118. In the chapter "Eresia, rifiuto équipe drammaturgica" in *Il teatro a Siena nel Cinquecento* cit., 135–180, Seragnoli suggests that there might be a correlation between the academics' view of a well-regulated society and the presence of heretics within the Academy itself (p. 162, note 82).
22 F. Cerreta, "Alessandro Piccolomini . . . " cit., 86–89. See also the

all important letter written to G. Spannocchi on January 11, 1561 and published in *Delizie delli eruditi bibliofili italiani* (Florence, 1865), 43–46; it is in this letter that Piccolomini makes a point of distancing himself from the *Intronati*'s theatrical activities.
23 M. Celse, "Alessandro Piccolomini .." cit., 63–66 and 73–74.
24 N. Borsellino and R. Mercuri, *Il teatro del Cinquecento* (Bari, 1973), 34.
25 F. Cerreta, "The Sienese manuscript of Bargagli's *Pellegrina*," *BHR*, XXX (1968), 601–616.
26 F. Cerreta, "Un nuovo autografo della *Pellegrina* di G. Bargagli: il manoscritto Patetta 357," *La bibliofilia*, LXXVI (1974), fasc. III, 224–239.
27 The letter is to be found in F. Cerreta, *La Pellegrina* cit., 14.
28 D. Seragnoli in "Eresia, rifiuto, équipe drammaturgica" cit., 135–180, analyses Piccolomini's involvement with the production of *L'Ortensio* and *La Pellegrina* (168–173) and concludes that at least one of the elements mentioned by Piccolomini—his twenty-five year old *désengagement* from the theatre—is only an hyperbole and utterly false; hence Cerreta should not rely too much on this particular calculation.
29 The letter to C. Saracini was first published by G. Milanesi, *Due lettere di A. Piccolomini senese* (Florence, 1878); for Sanesi's theory see note 20.
30 We can add that, though no name is mentioned, the play in question is definitely *La Pellegrina*; moreover, Piccolomini's undated letter points out that the commission for the writing of the play dates back to a few years before Ferdinando became Grand Duke since he is referred to as still being a cardinal.
31 N. Borsellino, "Il manoscritto della *Pellegrina*" cit., 107–111; Borsellino's argument had already appeared with the title "Una commedia del Cinquecento e la censura," *Problemi*, 1967, n.2, 88–93.
32 There are a couple of passages in Cerreta's edition which have caused me some perplexity in so far as the editor has chosen to accept Scipione's correction rather than Girolamo's original which can (but not always) be read under Scipione's erasure. Since I am working from a microfilm I can only suggest a partial solution to some of these points in question:
1) Act III, sc. ii—Cerreta does not restore in his edition after *muine*, cajolery (p. 137, l. 63) the following line: *e le sante co' paternostri*, and the saintly women with prayers.
2) Act III, sc. iii—*ad una [?] della comare*, to a [?] of my godmother, in the Sienese manuscript is read by Cerreta as *ad un monaco della chiesa*, to a monk of the church (p. 140, l. 88).
3) Act V, sc. iii—*cose che non importan un frullo*, things which aren't worth a cent (p. 188, l. 34); Cerreta keeps Scipione's *frullo*, a more literary term meaning 'nothing' (see *Decameron* II, 10: " . . . disse parole assai a Paganino, le quali non montavano un frullo" rather than the original and

legible *covelle*, a term with the same meaning and used in the *Decameron* by a Sienese (IX,4). There should be further paleographical research in some cases where numerous corrections have been made on the original script: Act I, sc. i, ii, v, vi; Act II, sc. vi, etc.; furthermore, the only two stage directions existing in the Sienese manuscript—Act III, sc. iii and Act V, sc. vi—seem to be written by two different hands. At the time I am writing these notes I have not been able to obtain a copy of the Patetta 357 manuscript in order to check if some of the erasures in the Sienese manuscript could have been made by Girolamo and not by Scipione; however, it appears that the last part of the penultimate repartee pronounced by Drusilla seems to be written by Scipione: Cerreta, however, decides, to include this passage in his edition (p. 207, l. 222–224).
33 F. Cerreta, *La Pellegrina* cit., 15. Despite the fact that Cerreta quotes from R. Galluzzi's *Storia del granducato di Toscana sotto il governo della casa Medici* (Florence, 1781, vol. II, 107), there is no evidence pointing to a formal or even popular acceptance of the title of Grand Duke prior to the official promulgation of December 13, 1569; in fact we have evidence that even four days earlier Cosimo was referred to as *Eccellenza* (see V. Maffei, *Dal titolo di duca di Firenze e Siena a Granduca di Toscana*, Florence, 1905, 67, note 2). Cosimo was crowned Grand Duke on March 5, 1570, a title which was recognised by the emperor only five years later.
34 F. Cerreta, "Un nuovo autografo . . . " cit., 230–239.
35 There are two further external factors which could be taken into consideration, but I feel that they do not add anything to either argument. The first is the mention of a Diet (Act V, sc. ii) which Cerreta believes to be that of Augsburg in 1566 (see F. Cerreta, *La Pellegrina* cit., 15) but it can be argued that in those years there had been a plethora of Diets and that Bargagli was not thinking of a particular Diet. Cerreta mentions (ibid., 15, note and 193, note 117), in connection with the clandestine weddings (Act V, sc. iv), that these were prohibited by the Tridentine Council with a ruling promulgated on May 1, 1564 (but this recommendation had been passed since August 7, 1563); since the contents of this decree were not widely known, Cerreta argues that Bargagli wouldn't have known of them in time to compose the play in 1564. I don't think that either of these historical situations can be used to establish a more precise dating of the play.
36 The letter has been published by G. Gori-Pannilini in *Lettere di Scipione Bargagli novelliere senese del secolo XVI* (Florence, 1865), 7–8.
37 N. Borsellino, "Il manoscritto della *Pellegrina*" cit., 111–119.
38 F. Cerreta, "The Sienese manuscript . . . " cit., 607.
39 Ibid., 608–609. Other anti-clerical remarks, clearly censored in the Sienese manuscript, reappear inexplicably in the *princeps* edition (see Borsellino,

"Una commedia del Cinquecento e la censura" cit., 90).
40 N. Borsellino, "Il manoscritto della Pellegrina" cit., 112.
41 F. Cerreta, "The Sienese manuscript . . . " cit., 608.
42 On this argument see also G.M. Cecchi's *Il Donzello* (Act I, sc. ii), *Gli Sciamiti* (Act I, sc. iv; Act II, sc. v and Act IV, sc. i).
43 F. Cerreta, *La Pellegrina* cit., 84, note 12.
44 This theme is mentioned by A. Staüble, "Una ricerca in corso: il personaggio del pedante nella commedia cinquecentesca," in *Il teatro italiano del Rinascimento* cit., 100–101.
45 For the dichotomy of the presentation of women characters in the *Intronati*'s works, see M.F. Piéjus, "Venus bifrons: le double idéal féminin dans *La Raffaella* d'Alessandro Piccolomini," in A. Rochon, ed., *Images de la femme dans la littérature italienne de la Renaissance* (Paris, 1980), 81–167; some interesting remarks on the topic are also to be found in the more recent volume edited by A. Rochon, *Au pays d'éros: littérature et érotisme en Italie de la Renaissance à l'âge baroque* (Paris, 1986).
46 It can be said that the original inspiration for this type of secret marriage is the *Decameron* (II, 3): for further information see G. Brucker, *Giovanni and Lusanna: love and marriage in Renaissance Florence* (London, 1985), especially the bibliography 123–135; I would like to thank Tim Nelson (Department of English, University of New England) for having shared with me his learned expertise and research on this topic. On Lucrezio's concurrent relationship to Drusilla and Lepida, K. Newman in "The politics of spectacle . . . " cit., 109, suggests that: "The pilgrimage itself is a metaphor for the journey toward self-understanding which Drusilla helps Lucrezio make, just as being thought married to the madwoman Lepida represents the suffering necessary before he can obtain Drusilla's love."
47 Boccaccio captures vividly another aspect of the monetary transactions in marriages in the story of Ricciardo da Chinzica (II, 10): here the old judge—well established and affluent—marries a young girl for sheer 'window dressing'; on the binomium eros-money, see K. Newman, "The politics of spectacle . . . " cit., 106–107.
48 For a thorough treatment of the *miles gloriosus* in sixteenth-century Italian theatre see D.C. Boughner, *The braggart in Italian Renaissance comedy* (Minneapolis, 1954).
49 F. Cerreta, *La Pellegrina* cit., 57–65.
50 Ibid., 19–21.
51 A. Mango, *La commedia in lingua nel cinquecento* (Florence, 1966), 237.
52 F. Cerreta, *La Pellegrina* cit., 22.
53 For a detailed study of the manuscripts of G.M. Cecchi's *Le Pellegrine* see my "Catalogo delle opere di G.M. Cecchi," *Studi e problemi di critica testuale* (October 1981), vol. 23, 39–75; the play is actually called *La*

Pellegrina in Baccio's list, 49. For a comprehensive evaluation of the play see my Doctorate of Philosophy thesis: *Le 'commedie osservate' di G.M. Cecchi* (Adelaide, 1974), 527–539.
54 F. Cerreta, *La Pellegrina* cit., 23–25.
55 Ibid., 25–30.
56 Ibid., 31.
57 S. Mamone, *Il teatro nella Firenze medicea* (Milan, 1981), 72, note 28.
58 M. Baratto, *La commedia del Cinquecento* (Vicenza, 1975), 144.
59 F. Cerreta, *La Pellegrina* cit., 31, note 2.
60 J. Vianey, "Deux sources inconnues de Rotrou," *Archives historiques, artistiques et littéraires*, II (1890–1891), 241–250; see also F. Cerreta, *La Pellegrina* cit., 31, note 3.
61 A.L. Stiefel, "Unbekannte italianische Quellem Jean Rotrou's," *Zeitschrift für französische Sprache und Literatur*, Suppl. V (1891), 1–39; see also F. Cerreta, *La Pellegrina* cit., 32, note 2.
62 F. Cerreta, *La Pellegrina* cit., 31, note 4.
63 Ibid., 32.
64 The letter concerning Bulgarini's project is partly reproduced by F. Cerreta, *La Pellegrina* cit., 46.
65 Given the very large bibliography existing on the 1589 festivities, we give here only the accounts of the festivities related specifically to *La Pellegrina* rather than the ones dealing with the pageantry and the processions which characterised this Medici wedding: G. Seriacopi, *Memorie e Ricordi 1588–1589*, Archivio di Stato di Firenze (Archivio del Magistrato de' Nove, filza 3679); G. Pavoni, *Diario descritto da Giuseppe Pavoni delle feste celebrate nelle solennissime Nozze delli Serenissimi sposi, il sig. Don Ferdinando Medici et la Signora Donna Christina di Loreno, Gran Duchi di Toscana . . .* (Bologna, 1589); S. Cavallino, *Raccolta di tutte le solennissime Feste nel Sponsalitio della Serenissima Gran Duchessa di Toscana fatte in Fiorenza il mese di Maggio 1589* (Rome, 1589); *Li sontuosissimi apparecchi. . . . Et la descrittione de gl'Intermedi rappresentati in una Comedia nobilissima recitata da gl'Intronati Senesi. . .* , Biblioteca Nazionale di Firenze (Palatino c.2.1.45); F. Settimani, *Diario fiorentino*, Archivio di Stato di Firenze (ms. 130). The last few years have seen the publication of a vast modern bibliography on sixteenth-century festivities; here are the main studies related to the 1589 wedding and to *La Pellegrina*: G. Bertelà and A. Petrioli Tofani, *Feste e apparati medicei da Cosimo I a Cosimo II* (Florence, 1969); L. Zorzi, *Il luogo teatrale a Firenze*, catalogue (Florence, 1975); L. Zorzi, *Il teatro e la città* (Turin, 1977), 63–224; V. Daddi Giovannozzi, "Di alcune incisioni dell'apparato per le nozze di Ferdinando de' Medici e Cristina di Lorena," *Rivista d'Arte*, XII, 1940, 87–100; P. Dearborn Massar, "A set of prints and a drawing for the 1589 Medici marriage festival," *Mas-*

ter Drawing 1 ; *Il potere e lo spazio. La scena del Principe*, catalogue (Florence, 1980), 332, 340 (note 3.19), 357 (notes 5.1–5.3); F. Ghisi, "Un aspect inédit des intermèdes de 1589 à la cour medicéenne," in *Les fêtes de la Renaissance* (Paris, 1956), 145–162; H. Purkis, "Les mascarades et les intermèdes florentins," in *Les fêtes de la Renaissance* (Paris, 1956), 246–251; M. Jacquot, "Les fêtes de Florence (1589). Quelques aspects de leur mise en scène," *Theatre Research*, III (1961), n. 6, 157–176; M. Jacquot, "Les fêtes du marriage de Ferdinand et de Christine de Loraine, Florence, 1589," in *Les fêtes de la Renaissance* (Paris, 1963); J. Laver, "Stage design for the Florentine Intermezzi of 1589," *Burlington Magazine*, vol. LX, 1932; A. Nagler, *Theatre festivals of the Medici* (New Haven and London, 1964), 70–92; F. Berti, "Studi su alcuni aspetti del diario inedito di Girolamo Seriacopi e sui disegni buontalentiani per i costumi del 1589," *Quaderni di teatro*, Anno II (1980), n.7, 157–168; H. Purkis, "Il rapporto tra gli intermedi e l'opera teatrale nell'Italia del sedicesimo secolo," *Letterature moderne*, Anno X (1960), fasc. 6, 806; S. Mamone, *Il teatro nella Firenze medicea* cit., 59–77; R. Strong, *Splendour at court* (London, 1973), 169–212; E. Cochrane, *Florence in the forgotten centuries* (Chicago, 1973).

66 The following are more specific historical and modern sources of information on the 1589 performances of *La Pellegrina*: *Quadernaccio di ricordi per conto della commedia*, Archivio di Stato di Firenze (Guardaroba medico, vol. 140); *Il potere e lo spazio*. cit., 340 (notes 3.22–3.23), 358 (notes 5.10–5.11), 358 (note 5.13), 364–367 (note 5.14); L. Zorzi, *Il luogo teatrale* cit., note 9.21; N. Pirrotta and E. Povoledo, *Li due Orfei* (Turin, 1969), 233–235; A. Warburg, "I costumi teatrali per gli intermezzi del 1589," in *Commemorazione della riforma melodrammatica* (Florence, 1895), 103–146.

67 Bastiano de' Rossi, *Descrizione dell'Apparato e gli Intermedi. Fatti per la Commedia rappresentata in Firenze* . . . (Florence, 1589).

68 C. Malvezzi, *Intermedi e concerti per la Commedia rappresentata in Firenze* . . . (Venice, 1591). For a more modern account of the music played in 1589 see the following: D.P. Walker, "Musique des intermèdes de *La Pellegrina*," in *Les fêtes de la Renaissance, 1589* (Paris, 1963), 1–157 [in this article Walker elaborates on "La musique des intermèdes florentins de 1589 et l'Humanisme," in *Les fêtes de la Renaissance* (Paris, 1956), 133–144]; U. Rolandi, "Emilio de' Cavalieri, il Granduca Ferdinando e l'Inferrigno," *Rivista musicale italiana*, XXVI (1929), 26; A. Solerti, *Gli albori del melodramma* (Florence, 1905), vol. II, 15 ff.; F. Testi, *La musica italiana nel Seicento. Il melodramma* (Milan, 1970), 11–105; F. Ghisi, *Feste musicali della Firenze Medicea, 1480–1589* (Florence, 1939). The only complete recording of the music of *La Pellegrina* is the one made by the Stockholm Chamber Choir on Emi Records, 1973; of the

several partial recordings of the *Pellegrina*'s *Intermedi*, a very interesting one is that of *Intermedi* two and six on Argo Stereo, 1970, ZRG 602 (*A Florentine Festival*). We are still to see a study of the 1589 Florentine production of the play in the context of the music and of the other spectacles performed at the royal wedding; such a study is outside the aim of the present introduction to the English translation of the play.
69 M. Florimi, in a note to his 1605 edition of the play, hints at performances in other Italian cities; F. Cerreta (*La Pellegrina* cit., 30, note 2) is sceptical of this piece of information. As I'm writing these notes I learn that on August 8, 1987 the *Accademia Musicale Chigiana* performed the *Intermezzi* of *La Pellegrina* at the end of the 44th *Settimana Musicale Senese*. The orchestra was under the direction of René Clemencic, the *Coro polifonico della Toscana* under the direction of Roberto Sabbiani and the *Coro d'opera della Chigiana* under the direction of Lajos Kozma. The performance followed the lines of the 1589 performance with the following adaptations: a narrator read Bastiano de' Rossi's description, the acts of *La Pellegrina* were read in an abbreviated form and during the performance of the *Intermezzi*, slides of Buontalenti's costumes and scenes were projected on a screen with the commentary of Elvira Zorzi; a similar performance is planned for the 1989 *Maggio Fiorentino*.
70 The *editio princeps* and seventeenth-century editions are described by F. Cerreta in *La Pellegrina* cit., 43–45 and 47–56 respectively.
71 Ibid., 51; the attribution is made by Allacci, Haym and the catalogue of the Bibliothèque Nationale de Paris.
72 Ibid., 52; the attribution is made by Allacci.
73 The play is included in the collection *Commedie degli Intronati*.

BIBLIOGRAPHY

Besides the works mentioned in the notes to the introduction, the following works on sixteenth century Italian theatre are important sources of historical information and reference material.

Apollonio, M., *Storia del teatro italiano*, Florence, 1981.
Bosisio, P., *Popolarità e classicità nel teatro comico del Cinquecento*, Milan, 1975.
Cagliaritano, U., *Vocabolario Sanese*, Florence, 1975.
Ferroni, G., *Il testo e la scena. Saggi sul teatro del Cinquecento*, Rome, 1980.
Greco, A., *Istituzione del teatro comico del Rinascimento*, Naples, 1976.
Mitchell, B., *Italian civic pageantry in the High Renaissance*, Florence, 1979.
Pandolfi, V., *Il teatro del Rinascimento e la Commedia dell'Arte*, Rome, 1969.
Sanesi, I., *La Commedia*, Milan, 1954.
Various Authors, *Il teatro classico italiano nel' 500*, Rome, 1971.

The Female Pilgrim

(LA PELLEGRINA)

a prose comedy

by DOCTOR GIROLAMO BARGAGLI

Materiale Intronato

To the magnanimous Prince, the most reverend and illustrious

SIGNOR DON FERDINANDO

CARDINAL DE' MEDICI

SCIPIONE BARGAGLI'S UNPUBLISHED DEDICATORY LETTER

To the most serene Signor Don Ferdinando de' Medici

Grand Duke of Tuscany

my most revered Lord and master.

Messer Girolamo Bargagli's particular service to your Serene Highness, while working as a judge in Florence, did indeed gain your favour for, as he was about to return home, you ordered him to compose a play for you personally. Perhaps it was because of the proofs you had already had of his talent that you thought him capable of it. Apart from his serious legal studies, in which he made constant progress—as he showed both in the Civil and Criminal Courts of Genoa—there was the nature of his intellectual pursuits in his own city. There he carried out academic studies in the School of the Intronati, especially in the field of imaginative writing—so that he could be considered reasonably capable of satisfying your wishes, as well as being anxious, and feeling obliged, to do so. The resulting play—superbly composed by him and presented to Your Highness, and (from what I hear) kindly received by you—was meant to become your personal property and, as such (unless special permission should be given), not to be touched in any way.

After he died, I found recently among his other compositions this very play, called *The Female Pilgrim,* and, realizing that it was written for you, I was anxious to offer it to you at once, as I now do in all humility. I do so on an occasion[1] which, we all hope and pray to the Lord, will have a happy and joyful ending like that which we expect from the plot of a good comedy. For this reason, Your Highness, do not disdain this production. Indeed, I don't think you can disdain it, for it is one of your own fruits and one which once pleased you. (Things produced by private persons in the service of great princes are customarily called their fruits.) Things in the material world grow in the same way, being born in places in this lower world by the action of the powerful and beneficent rays of the heavenly sun.

You will forgive any possible defects which there might be because of the sudden death of the author just when he was blooming and coming to his peak. For this reason I beg you to show your most benign graces to a creature born after his father's death.[2] He, carrying his father's name, also carries (and so do his uncles, Doctor Celso from Macerata University and myself), a heart wholly devoted to Your Serene Highness on whom may God bestow the prosperity and happiness that he deserves and most desires.

From Siena the fourth day of March 1587.[3]

> Your Serene Highness, I remain
> your most humble and devout servant,
>
> SCIPION BARGAGLI

[SCIPIONE BARGAGLI'S LETTER PUBLISHED IN THE 1589 *PRINCEPS* EDITION]

To the most serene Don Ferdinando de' Medici,
Grand Duke of Tuscany,

my most revered Lord and master.

No greater or more worthy or dearer reward could have been wished by my brother, Doctor Girolamo, for his labour (undertaken by wish of Your Serene Highness who commissioned the play) than the one he would have today, were he among us, in seeing that the play he composed has been chosen, from a great number of excellent comic works, by you and your most talented men of letters, to be worthy of being performed on the occasion of a wedding, of a royal wedding, indeed of your own wedding (as we have seen) and in seeing that the play met with the joyous approval of the people observing the festivities. It is as if this play with its happy ending (and despite the delays and difficulties not of your making, which might have prevented it being performed at all) symbolised or foreboded a similar happy event, namely your most longed-for wedding. No doubt that is why Your

Highness has seen fit for the play to be performed with all the pomp and with the most splendid and appropriate decorations that could have been chosen from your rich collection or could have been constructed by craftsmen. How magnificent were the proscenium and especially the intermezzi which proved a fitting ornament to such a play.

The seed of this masterpiece was first provided by Your Highness who sowed it and cultivated it in the fertile imagination of the author; once it was fully grown, it was displayed to the whole world in this wonderful theatre. It is soon to appear for the first time in the new medium of print; it is a well known fact that many highly regarded personalities have wanted to see it published. I have no doubts that it will return to You, from whom it first came, hoping that the play will now (as on the occasion of its performance) be benignly accepted and enjoyed by You in this new printed form. You have already given a similar indication of your natural benevolence by accepting and delighting in the emblem of the king of bees in the middle of his swarm with the motto "Maiestate Tantum."[4] That emblem was invented by me to express a special quality in which your Serene Highness resembles that little insect: you do not have, or you do not ever use, the sting towards your subjects, but you always appear secure and protected inside the shield of your majesty. Equally you think that every weapon, every shelter, every defence, every possible way of preserving Yourself and your Tuscan realm rests with you alone and with your natural regality. Obviously such self-assurance and boldness is justified principally by the sheer benevolence, the sincere love, the clear consideration and the due reverence continuously offered to You by your most faithful and devout subjects. All this affection which is born in them because of your natural and loving fondness is to be compared to that of the shepherd towards his flock or, rather, that of the father towards his dear family. This conforms with the advice of Agasicles, king of the Lacedaemonians: on being asked how a prince could be sure of his life without being forever guarded, he replied: "He should rule over his people and subjects as a father does over his own children." The device mentioned above has been engraved on the reverse side of your highest denomination gold coins, just as on the obverse there appears a picture of Your majesty in full armour.

I thank Your Serene Highness for having granted me these two favours and I do so in the most proper way I can; I kneel most humbly before You.

From Siena, the 17th day of September 1589.

Your Serene Highness, I remain
your most humble and devout servant,

SCIPION BARGAGLI

DRAMATIS PERSONAE

CASSANDRO	an old gentleman
LEPIDA	his daughter
GIGLIETTA	Lepida's nurse
MESSER TERENZIO	a young man posing as a tutor
TARGHETTA	Cassandro's male servant
DRUSILLA	a young pilgrim
RICCIARDO	her male companion
LUCREZIO	a young man
CARLETTO	his servant
MESSER FEDERIGO	a German student
CAVICCHIA	his servant
VIOLANTE	an innkeeper
BARGELLO	police officer

ACT I

SCENE I

CASSANDRO, an old gentleman; GIGLIETTA, nurse

CASSANDRO: Listen here Giglietta. Because of Lepida's prolonged and strange illness, I have resolved on two things: first we must convince her prospective husband that it's just a minor complaint and, second, we must keep it quiet and a secret as long as it is possible. If anyone were to spread a rumour about the strange dizziness she keeps getting, we would soon have a horde of women descending on us, all babbling their opinions.

GIGLIETTA: I just wish I could cure my poor mistress of her illness! Meanwhile I'm happy to help her and not mention her state to anyone.

CASSANDRO: This has been a real calamity. At such an awkward time! Instead of having a house full of caterers and cooks, I find myself having to send for doctors and druggists. I want her seen to straight away. An illness can usually be cured if it's checked in time. Go up to Lepida's room, while I fetch Maestro Lazzaro to look her over.

GIGLIETTA: That's all we need! Why be in such a hurry to call doctors and take tests?[5] Isn't it better to wait and see for a while longer? There's always a chance that this illness will disappear by itself.

CASSANDRO: We've already waited two days! I don't want any more delays.

GIGLIETTA: Master, don't meddle with medicines and doctors. If Lepida is really a little off her head, they'll only make her stark mad: I've seen that happen often enough in my days. These donkey-riders[6] don't really know which way to turn, except in the case of malaria and colds. This illness of Lepida's is something out of the way. It's making her melancholy[7] and contrary. She wants to contradict everyone and everything. Let it be. It may run its own course.

CASSANDRO: What do you mean by 'melancholy'? I don't see why she should be melancholy. She surely can't be grieving because I chose her a husband who isn't to her liking. She hasn't had an old man, or a cripple, or a deformed husband chosen for her, as other girls have. I haven't given her away to a wandering doctor, or to a penniless knight, or to an impoverished courtier, or to a count without a county or to a two-bit merchant without any cash: I've betrothed her to a young man who's handsome, noble, rich, well brought up and with the best of attributes.

GIGLIETTA: True enough. But from the moment the groom came the other evening to visit her, from that . . . blessed moment, Lepida hasn't been herself. I'm afraid she's been put under a spell and that some wicked woman, some ex-girl-friend of the groom, has bewitched her.

CASSANDRO: What do you mean, 'bewitched'? The moment you women hear of an unusual illness, you start thinking of witchcraft.

GIGLIETTA: I certainly hope this practice of witchcraft can be rooted out. All the same, you just wouldn't believe how many people practice witchcraft. Master, if you only knew how much that poor girl suffers at night, you'd agree with me. She seems to be all right in the day time because she keeps herself occupied. But last night, truly, she had dreadful fits. She got all bloated and kept on getting out of bed, throwing her arms about and making strange noises. I nearly called you two or three times. As I didn't know what else to do I went and lit a candle and started reciting prayers: the holy epistle, Saint Giuliano's prayer,[8] the *Qui habitet* and the *Salvia regina*. Then I made the sign of the cross all around the bed. And believe it or not this quietened her down a bit.

CASSANDRO: Look here nurse, all this madness and strange behaviour could be spirits: they play such tricks. You'll see that's all it is.

GIGLIETTA: Do you really believe in spirits?

CASSANDRO: Why not? The Gospel mentions them, right?

GIGLIETTA: [*Aside*] I think I'll go along with his idea of the spirits to stop him calling the doctor.

CASSANDRO: What did you say?

GIGLIETTA: If they are spirits we're talking about, then there's no need for the doctor.

CASSANDRO: There are doctors for these illnesses too—priests trained in exorcising spirits. Now that I think of it, there's a holy man in the monastery nearby who, in my days, has performed many a miracle in driving away spirits. I'll go and see him.
GIGLIETTA: Let's wait a bit longer, master; there's always time for that.
CASSANDRO: No, no, I don't want to be kept in suspense any longer. I must find help or advice somewhere. I've heard that it's easy to get rid of spirits if they're discovered in time but that the task is much harder if they've settled in. I wouldn't want my future son-in-law to grow suspicious. Go back upstairs while I go and see Don Marcello—that's the name of that monk—to ask him if he can visit my daughter.
GIGLIETTA: If you insist. But make sure this monk behaves. I've seen these exorcists abuse the wretched souls placed in their care. They are pitiless in breaking their wills. I wouldn't want to see Lepida beaten up. She's such a delicate creature.[9]
CASSANDRO: If she doesn't snap out of the state she's in, she's done for. I'll do whatever's necessary, there's no time to waste. Don't leave my daughter alone and make sure she doesn't leave her room. [*Exit*]
GIGLIETTA: Don't worry! This spirit isn't one to be scared by holy water. [*Aside*] Lord alive, what passion and spirit this girl has shown; the mess she's got herself into because of love! Let's hope it all turns out well.

SCENE II

MESSER TERENZIO, a young man posing as a tutor; GIGLIETTA, a nurse

MESSER TERENZIO: [*Aside*] Where has the nurse disappeared to so early in the day? The way things are at present, she shouldn't ever leave Lepida alone. Ah, here she is.—Giglietta, where have you been? You know very well that while Lepida is pretending to be mad, she shouldn't be left alone.
GIGLIETTA: What else could I do? The old man called me downstairs in the street. He'd have fetched the doctor if I hadn't talked him out of it.
MESSER TERENZIO: The doctor? That would have been disastrous. A doctor would probably have made her ill with some concoction or

wrong prescription. Besides, by examining her urine and checking other symptoms, he'd have discovered her pregnancy, and that's exactly what we're trying to hide.
GIGLIETTA: Now you see why I had to get the idea out of the old man's head. But I wasn't so successful with another thing.
MESSER TERENZIO: What thing?
GIGLIETTA: He's got it in his head to call some monk to find out whether she's possessed by spirits.
MESSER TERENZIO: I don't like that idea. Some of those individuals are quite cunning. He might discover something.
GIGLIETTA: Too true. I'm still shaking all over. But we ought to have expected it. Cassandro's a rich man, with only one boy and one girl who's the apple of his eye. He's organizing his daughter's wedding, and right in the middle of it all she falls prey to an unusual illness. Wouldn't he do his utmost to have her cured? What a mess we got ourselves into by faking this madness of hers. As far as I'm concerned, I never liked the situation: you only seem to have wasted a lot of time without any results. You could have let the marriage her father arranged go ahead. Even if she was married, Lepida would have still given herself to you and only you.
MESSER TERENZIO: What? Do you expect me to share her with somebody else?
GIGLIETTA: Surely you know that the husband's 'share' doesn't mean anything. Husbands are only good to carry out errands and make things easier for people in love. It's the husband's duty to pay bills and buy clothes; all the hassles, quarrels and troubles in a woman's life are for the husbands while the pleasures, caresses and good moods are for the lovers. It's just like what a curate of ours used to say: he had to celebrate mass while somebody else got all the benefits.
MESSER TERENZIO: One way or another husbands will take their pleasure with their wives. But love can't be shared; sharing it means destroying it.
GIGLIETTA: I don't know anything about that. When I was young, I used to share my love around and I never had any complaints.
MESSER TERENZIO: Giglietta, this isn't the time for idle chat. I'm just telling you this: if a man loves a girl, he shouldn't let her get married to somebody else. He may think before the wedding that he's in control of her feelings, but all that daily contact with her

husband and sleeping together at night time can easily alter her affection. And besides these distractions at home, there are others outside: the chance to visit many places, to go to parties and banquets, to collect admirers, to be praised by one and flattered by another; all of this puts ideas in a woman's head. It makes her haughty, and she forgets her former lover. Though I must say that I consider myself a husband rather than a lover, since she is already my wife, as you know.
GIGLIETTA: Exactly. But I was the only witness when you married. It was done between ourselves, and you can be sure that I'll never utter a word.
MESSER TERENZIO: That's true what you say about our wedding; not only love but also fairness and duty all indicate that she shouldn't belong to anyone else.
GIGLIETTA: Do you think she'd be the one to be first secretly married to one man and then publicly married to another? Messer Terenzio, I fear that, in trying to have her all to yourself, you may lose her completely. I never thought this scheme would work, and now it must fail. Firstly, Lepida can't go on with this masquerade much longer (and if she's found out then she'll be disowned by her father for ever); secondly, even if she manages to keep up her pretence, what will come of it? If this fiancé rejects her publicly, she'll never find anyone else who'll want her. Even if you revealed everything to the father he wouldn't give her to you. He despises you because he thinks you're only a poor private tutor. As for you, you'll soon be called back home, and the poor girl will be left behind with her reputation ruined. Do as I say. Don't make her go on feigning madness. Let her marry this man Lucrezio, and let me take care of things. If they don't turn out sweet and rosy, then you can take it out on me.
MESSER TERENZIO: Look here, Lepida is mine and I won't share her with anybody else. Besides, if we don't follow this scheme through, how will we handle the pregnancy? Can't you see that this way she is keeping the groom at a distance so that he can't start any horseplay and discover her swollen belly?
GIGLIETTA: Well, since that's the way you feel about it, let's let things ride. But I must tell you again that my heart isn't in it since I can't see how things will come to a head.
MESSER TERENZIO: Nurse, I can see that Lepida hasn't told you about the scheme we worked out together last night.

GIGLIETTA: She hasn't told me a word. Perhaps because she hasn't had the time.
MESSER TERENZIO: I'd better do it myself then. I've told you many times how noble and rich I am at home. And how, on my journey home, I stopped here and fell in love with Lepida and decided to take up a job in this house as a tutor to Rutilio[10] under the name Terenzio.
GIGLIETTA: I know all that and I also know that your real name is Lucrezio: when Lepida and I want to talk without being understood by others, she takes pleasure in calling you by this name. But what's all this leading up to?
MESSER TERENZIO: The point is that since I found myself so quickly and unexpectedly involved with Lepida, and in such conditions, I decided to write home to my father, if he's still alive, and to my family so that they can send written proof of my wealth and nobility. Once I receive this, and once Lepida is turned away from her present fiancé (as she will be), I intend to reveal myself to Cassandro, hoping that then he won't object to my marrying Lepida. That's why we have to go on with this masquerade for a few days longer until the testimonials and the answers arrive. Meanwhile the wedding with this other chap must be stopped. Once we've revealed our agreement to the old man, and he has ascertained how far things have gone, he'll have to make the best of it.
GIGLIETTA: Since that's how things are, let's go ahead as planned. But I beg you to take care of Lepida. You see how much she's doing out of love for you. Don't desert her.
MESSER TERENZIO: Desert her? I'd rather die. Go on up to her room.
GIGLIETTA: Aren't you coming too? Since the old man's out, you could come and comfort her at your leisure.
MESSER TERENZIO: I can't, I've come out to post these letters and to look for Lucrezio. I want to get him talking to find out how he's reacting to this 'madness'! I'll try to get away myself before the old man comes back. You know a miser can't stay away too long from where he keeps his treasure.
GIGLIETTA: Spoken like a scholar![11] Who wouldn't fall in love with you! [*Goes upstairs*]

SCENE III

MESSER TERENZIO alone

How true is the proverb that says Fortuna is fickle! I can testify to that better than anybody else. Many years ago I was well off and living happily in my home town. All of a sudden I was made prisoner and held as a slave for a long time. Again I was freed quite unexpectedly and treated with every kindness and consideration. I was happily on my way home when I came to this town and fell in love. Love has changed all my plans and has made me put on the vulgar clothes worn by pedants. Now just when I thought that Fortuna had repented and relented towards me, since she had been so favourable in making me fall in love, she turns on me and persecutes me again; at the thought of this wedding all the joys I have tasted so far turn sour. With this scheme which I had worked out, I hoped to insure my happiness before the old man could marry Lepida to anybody else, and my wretched luck has brought the threat of this wedding upon me. But why do you complain, Lucrezio? Even if it should end now, hasn't your past success in love been enough to keep you happy forever? How will you ever forget the moment when, after having been accepted and loved by everyone in the family, you started reading, to bide the time during the summer heat, either Amadigi's or Don Florisello's[12] adventures? You could see her become interested in love, and with a word here and a word there you were soon getting greater favours from her than those usually allowed to a courteous tutor? Oh when I remember how sweetly I disclosed my thoughts to her for the first time! Love had tied up my tongue with more knots than it had done with my heart. I couldn't reveal my feelings in my own words and so, obeying her father's directions in teaching her to write, one day when we were left alone I wrote two lines on a separate sheet, telling her who I was and what I had set out to do to serve her. In handing the paper to her I said: "Take this sample and learn it for the future." She read it, uttered no word, turned pale and, eyeing me twice from head to toe, put it among the other papers and took it to her room. Oh what a beautiful beginning to my happy times! I won't mention all the other pleasures that followed and that have flowed on until recently; as they

are unmentionable, they will remain unspoken and relegated to
my thoughts. I admit that the memory of such great bliss should
keep a lover happy forever. But alas, I also know that lovers'
wishes are endless. The sweetness in the past makes my present
difficulty even more bitter. But I don't want to lose all hope since
two people in love proverbially overcome all difficulties. I'm only
sorry that Lepida, in feigning madness, might think she's giving
proof of a loftier love, forgetting that I have to masquerade as a
pedant. God only knows how painful it is for me to wear these
clothes, to check my gait, to put on a facade, to say things worthy
only of Polyphilus,[13] in brief to lose my own identity. But what
am I saying? Didn't Jupiter[14] turn into a bull and into a swan
in order to assuage his love? Now I find myself even muttering
some pedantries, so much am I getting used to playing this role!
I'd better be off since I'm delaying doing what I came out to do.
The fact that I can't unburden myself to anyone makes me carry
on more than I should. [*Exit*]

SCENE IV

LUCREZIO, a young man; CARLETTO, his servant

LUCREZIO: Well, Carletto, a fellow never gets much out of something
he does against his will.
CARLETTO: Very true, master. I've always been poor against my
wishes and I've never got anything out of it. Your situation certainly
deserves sympathy; but I can't see what good can come
out of breaking your engagement so suddenly. Breach of promise
always causes bad feeling. The wisest thing is either not to get
engaged at all or else, if you do, to go through with it and put up
with the consequences.
LUCREZIO: If only I had got to hear of her madness sooner. I'm sure
it must have been known for quite a while.
CARLETTO: It's your own fault that you didn't find out enough about
her. All the same, it's odd that when someone has to hire a maid
for the house, even if she's to stay only four days, he tries to take
a good look at her and learn everything possible about her; but,
when one takes a wife, who's going to be a companion for the rest
of one's life and on whom the well being of the whole household
will depend, one accepts her and takes her without looking at

her, blindfolded, as you would say. You've been a merchant, you know that if you buy goods without checking them first, you'll find some rotten ones.
LUCREZIO: You're right, but the deed's done now and I don't know what I can do about it.
CARLETTO: I've already told you, master; the last thing you must do is to knock her back.
LUCREZIO: Do you want me to put up with a mad wife?
CARLETTO: Where will you find any woman who's not a bit daft or lightheaded? Anyway, are you really sure that she's insane?
LUCREZIO: Insane or possessed or something of the kind. She behaves in very strange ways. You should have seen her last night when I went to visit her! What do you want me to do with a woman who's possessed?
CARLETTO: Do you think you'll ever meet a woman who's not somehow devilish? Let's not mention the ones who are so ugly that they actually look like the devil. Even the beautiful ones have a bit of the devil either in their eyes, or on their cheeks, or in their bosoms, or on their mouths, or in their hands, or in the way they dance or in the way they sing. Tell me a gesture, a movement which doesn't reveal the presence of a tempting devil! I think hell is full of them. I won't mention those who are a bit devilish in their heads or in their brains. Others still, like your future wife, are devilish in another manner and perhaps in a more excusable one since, in this case, they are the tormented ones while in the other cases they are the tormenters.
LUCREZIO: Carletto, you shouldn't make fun of something that's so important.
CARLETTO: I know how important it is; but what I want to say is that I'm afraid Fortuna has put you in this predicament out of sheer vindictiveness.
LUCREZIO: What for?
CARLETTO: Because you have been knocking back so many good matches that have been arranged for you. You know, that can happen to those like you who have played hard to get and upset so many prospective weddings: "I don't want this one; that one's known to be ugly; that one is short; that one has a small dowry; I don't like that one's relatives; I don't know enough about this one's social standing; this one wouldn't know how to run a household because she was educated in a nunnery; the mother of that

one had a bad reputation"; then, they end up empty-handed.
LUCREZIO: I'm sure that this is some sort of vendetta or punishment meted out by my fate, but for another reason and of deeper significance than you think.
CARLETTO: What could that be? Your life, as far as I know, doesn't deserve such a punishment.
LUCREZIO: I deserve it more than you think. I'm guilty of a sin which is continuously troubling my conscience.
CARLETTO: I'm flabbergasted.
LUCREZIO: What is a greater offence than an omission in diligence and faithfulness which has caused the death of the very person for whom, above anybody else, I wished everything in life?
CARLETTO: I'm speechless. Please, share this secret with me, if I'm worthy of it.
LUCREZIO: I'll tell you the story, though I'm still upset at the thought of it. You'll understand that the reason why I've been loath to take a wife until now isn't due to my being too fussy.
CARLETTO: Please, do tell me the whole story; I'm longing to hear it.
LUCREZIO: You know that three years ago I returned from Valencia where I'd spent two years looking after the Lanfranchis' business.[15]
CARLETTO: Of course I know it. I entered your service just after you got back.
LUCREZIO: Well now, hear this: I had just arrived in Valencia when Fortuna placed before me a neighbour of mine, as beautiful and attractive a girl as you would ever see; I fell in love with her straightaway and since I kept on seeing her all the time—either as she was sewing by the window or as she was watering the violets she kept on the balcony—my love grew so strong that I could find no rest. Love smiled upon me, since as soon as she became aware of my passion she seemed to want to compete with me in showing her feelings.
CARLETTO: That was certainly a good start, and the end should be even better. Where love is returned, one should find only bliss.
LUCREZIO: Listen now. Despite the ardent love she bore for me, despite all my entreaties and all the opportunities I created, I could only get from her a few passionate words. I didn't go beyond kissing her beautiful hand, since she insisted that she'd rather die loving me than satisfy me while losing her honour. And at times she'd say: "Have pity on your Drusilla—for that was her name—since Love forces her to extreme pains and her integrity forbids her

to seek any remedy to them." In short, since I didn't manage to storm that citadel either through threats or machinations or battle or siege, I was only left with the option of lawful possession. So I agreed to marry her. As I was being offered what I hadn't even hoped for in my wildest dreams, I married her secretly, and voluntarily I drew up a contract for my happiness.

CARLETTO: And so you got what you wanted?

LUCREZIO: In fact, no. She told me that even now it wasn't proper for me to possess her as a husband unless I made our marriage public in the proper manner.

CARLETTO: Why did you marry her secretly? Why didn't you come out in the open?

LUCREZIO: Because of certain reasons which would take me too long to explain, this is what was thought proper. But by this means I only managed to obtain one kiss as a pledge of her love.

CARLETTO: You are telling the story of a great love and of a woman's great integrity.

LUCREZIO: That's exactly how it all went. These things had barely taken place when I was recalled to Italy by my employers. Only those who have found themselves in similar predicaments can imagine how sad I was to go. But since I had to comply with my orders, I gave her my word of honour that I would return within one year. Once in Pisa, just as I was about to get everything settled, I was told that some of my business associates had gone bunkrupt and that others had died. Two years went by before I could leave and then, when everything was arranged and I was about to leave, who should arrive here from Valencia but Fabrizio, a native of Lucca, an intimate friend of mine who knew about the marriage and who brought me news that will make me unhappy forever.

CARLETTO: What news? Had she married somebody else?

LUCREZIO: Alas, he brought me the sad news of her death; and since I didn't die straightaway at learning this, I don't think it's ever possible to die of grief.

CARLETTO: What a dreadful thing. No wonder, the moment this man from Lucca arrived, you left suddenly for the country villa where you wandered through the woods bellowing like a bull. I remember you stayed there in that mood for more than two months on end without giving any reason for it.

LUCREZIO: Don't you remember that I told you it was because of a

great loss I'd sustained?
CARLETTO: Yes sir, but I thought you talked of a trading loss.
LUCREZIO: If only it had been! A material loss wouldn't have made me grieve for more than two days.
CARLETTO: Was the news brought by the man from Lucca reliable?
LUCREZIO: Yes. In fact, the night before he left Valencia, having learned of her death, he went (out of love for me) to see her and saw her on a bier while they were making the funeral arrangements. This will make me unhappy for the rest of my life because, had I returned to Valencia as promised, Drusilla wouldn't have died. It was her suffering for my delayed return that killed her. I have murdered my beloved.
CARLETTO: Certainly, my lord, you had good reason to grieve: I believe that to lose one's beloved is the greatest pain one can bear in life. I don't like the attitude of those who say that women are animals which are only good when young and alive, but are worth nothing when old and dead so that, if a lady dies, her man doesn't think twice about seeking a new companion. But you shouldn't torment yourself over things that can't be remedied, nor become prey to desperation. Now that she's tragically dead, because you couldn't go back to her in time (though you had every intention of doing so), what can you do? Why should you feel any remorse?
LUCREZIO: I too have tried to find some consolation by arguing this way. To help me resign myself, I let my relatives persuade me the other day, after long opposition, to take a wife. But this will never banish the memory of Drusilla from my heart.
CARLETTO: If you do this, you'll have taken a new wife out of desperation.
LUCREZIO: That's true, you can say that I've taken her out of desperation, and a wife like this one will make me live in despair for ever if I don't try to free myself from her. So help me to think of a way to carry out my resolution.
CARLETTO: Don't act rashly. This madness[16] of hers may not be congenital, it may only be momentary and pass off. Isn't it worthwhile enquiring about it?
LUCREZIO: Whether this ailment is old or new, momentary or not, people would always say I'd married a madwoman. What other information do you need?
CARLETTO: Well, if you find that this is an illness dating way back, you could reject her much more easily, if you don't want to go

ahead with the marriage.
LUCREZIO: That's a good point. I want my doctor to visit her and in the meantime you might extract some information from Targhetta.
CARLETTO: I'll do it deftly and conscientiously. Now, I recall that a pilgrim came to take up lodgings in Violante's house four days ago; they say she's an astrologer, a soothsayer, a charlatan, almost a fairy.
LUCREZIO: How do you know all this?
CARLETTO: I heard it from Violante herself since, as you know, she's my friend and she's told me quite a bit about how this girl can diagnose and cure serious illnesses. It's true that I haven't concentrated on the details.
LUCREZIO: What's certain is that some hidden illnesses of women can only be uncovered by other women. It wouldn't be a bad idea for you to learn if this pilgrim can help us with this illness.
CARLETTO: I'd better go and see Violante without further delay.
LUCREZIO: You'd better go on the other errand I've given you first and then do this one. [*Exit Carletto*] Meanwhile I'll go to the Ponte[17] to see if the ships which I expected from Marseilles have arrived. Here's Cassandro. I want to find out from him how things are going and at the same time tell him of my resolution.

SCENE V

CASSANDRO, LUCREZIO

CASSANDRO: [*Aside*] This Don Marcello is certainly an exceptional old man and a venerable monk. If there were more people like him, the world would be a better place to live in. How unlucky he is to suffer from that ailment which immobilises him for days on end, as is the case now.
LUCREZIO: [*Aside*] He must have gone to hear mass from those monks; they officiate very well.
CASSANDRO: [*Aside*] In brief, "Old clothes come undone at the seams." When we are getting on in years, we are full of aches and pains. Since he cannot make it to my place as I had intended, I shall have to send Lepida there; he's been very kind and compassionate towards me.
LUCREZIO: [*Aside*] I must speak to him.—Good day, Messer Cassandro.

CASSANDRO: I'm glad to see you, my son. Anything new?
LUCREZIO: Nothing new. I was going to ask after Lepida.
CASSANDRO: According to nurse she hasn't spent a good night; but all day yesterday, she was fine. In the daytime she gets by fairly well; it's in the night that she suffers. That makes me think that her ailment is nothing but fear which grows stronger during the night; I do hope it will pass in a few days' time. What really upsets me is the trouble this is causing you and the disruption to the wedding plans. I do want it to be a beautiful and festive occasion; we certainly will find a remedy to send away this ailment.
LUCREZIO: It's difficult to find a remedy for anything deeply-rooted.
CASSANDRO: You hurt me very much if you imply that this may be a congenital disease. I'm not so crazy as to give away my wealth for her dowry if I felt sure I had an unhealthy daughter. To do so would only bring shame upon me. If that had been the case, wouldn't I have made her enter a nunnery? Nunneries today, as a friend of mine likes to say, have taken the place of the labyrinths of yesteryear: they are used to imprison monsters. If I'd been able to hide this tragedy, why would I have shared my unhappiness with others? Why would I have brought this dishonour on myself? I assure you that until three days ago Lepida was as fresh as a rose, wise as a Sibyl. Just ask the neighbours.
LUCREZIO: One shouldn't pay attention to them; it's well known that young girls, while still in their fathers' care, are all beautiful, kind, angel-like, able to rule a kingdom, but the moment they are married all these qualities vanish.
CASSANDRO: Tell me, didn't you enquire about her first, weren't you given any information?
LUCREZIO: Who will ever speak evil of girls who are to be married? Don't you know the great scruples people have about telling the truth? They say: One shouldn't deprive a young girl of her good fortune. They don't think of saying: We're bringing misfortune on a young man.
CASSANDRO: The misfortune came after, as everyone can testify.
LUCREZIO: Are you implying that I'm the cause of it?
CASSANDRO: I'm not saying that, Lucrezio; on the contrary, I'm glad you're the one who's marrying her and I am proud of you, since I love you as I love my son Rutilio. What I'm saying is that the cause of this evil is recent and, for this very reason, it will be easy to find a remedy. That's why I've just gone to see a very

exceptional monk, my friend.
LUCREZIO: What do monks have to do with these evils?
CASSANDRO: Let me tell you. After thinking over my daughter's illness, and her behaviour, I have begun to think that it could be a case of evil spirits. This monk is very knowledgeable in these matters and the moment Lepida appears before him, he'll know whether she's possessed by some spirit or not. And if it is a case of evil spirits, he will exorcise her. If it's not, we'll look for other remedies.
LUCREZIO: In other words, my future wife has to go around churches to be exorcised and to be maligned by people? How will we ever keep this story quiet? And finally you'll forgive me Messer Cassandro if I. . . .
CASSANDRO: What do you mean "if I"?
LUCREZIO: That's enough. I think that anyone who hears of this story will forgive me.
CASSANDRO: Explain what you mean. I don't understand.
LUCREZIO: I shall speak frankly. I can't bear to think that people will say Lucrezio Lanfranchi has married a madwoman or a woman possessed or, at least, without all her mental faculties.
CASSANDRO: I tell you she hasn't ever been ill before. She'll recover.
LUCREZIO: It's bad enough that people will always be able to say in the future that she has been ill and, as far as I'm concerned, I cannot chase from my mind the thought that she was always ill.
CASSANDRO: If I can convince you that this is only a three-day old sickness and that tomorrow she'll be well again, what will you say?
LUCREZIO: When I see this then we'll talk again. But I know this much: when a door once comes off its hinges it won't ever go back into place as it was before.
CASSANDRO: Lucrezio, I've always thought you sensible, the sort of person who always behaves as befits a nobleman like you.
LUCREZIO: And I've always thought you a person who demands honesty from everybody. I'll take leave now since I have some business to do.
CASSANDRO: Off you go, then, and remember to come this evening to visit your betrothed. [*Exit Lucrezio*] I don't like the way he spoke to me. But I didn't want to argue with him as I don't want to antagonise him, especially since it's quite understandable that he should be upset. Meanwhile, before anything else, I want to

find out whether he still has the right to reject her since he has only asked for her hand but hasn't given her the ring. Alas, I hope we haven't reached the stage where I'll have to take legal action against him, as has happened in other cases. I'd better call Giglietta to tell her to take Lepida to the abbey. [*Calls*]

SCENE VI

CASSANDRO, GIGLIETTA, TARGHETTA, Cassandro's servant

CASSANDRO: Giglietta, can't you hear me, Giglietta?
GIGLIETTA: [*Upstairs*] Master?
CASSANDRO: Come down here.
GIGLIETTA: [*Upstairs*] Straightaway. Oh, I can't go up and down like I used to. I just can't, and to think that once I used to do it all the time. Can't you tell me from down there what you want?
CASSANDRO: No, you foolish woman. Do you want the whole neighbourhood to hear my business?
GIGLIETTA: [*Upstairs*] Do you want me to bring down your account book[18] as you often ask me, or do you just want me down there?
CASSANDRO: I'll give you a good thrashing if you don't shut up and come down. Come down as you are, since you don't have to go anywhere yet. Hurry and send down Targhetta too.
GIGLIETTA: [*Upstairs*] You always want us to run an errand together, as a duet.[19]
CASSANDRO: I'd rather have you both dead and buried.
GIGLIETTA: [*Upstairs*] In that case he'd better come down first.
CASSANDRO: You're a real nincompoop. Come down, I say. [*Aside*] If only this monk would exorcise her he'd relieve my heart of a great burden: in the past two days the household has been overcome by gloom. Even the tutor, who has nothing to do with the matter, shows signs of it.
GIGLIETTA: [*Comes down*] Here I am, master.
CASSANDRO: At last! Tell me, was it you who told me that Lepida feels better in the daytime than at night and that at noon she's so calm, and for such a long spell, that one wouldn't think that she's sick?
GIGLIETTA: Yes sir, why?
CASSANDRO: I've been to see Don Marcello and I've found him unwell because of his cold; since he can't come here we have to take

Lepida to him. To avoid any further commotion and the need to call other women, I thought you should take her at the time when she feels at her best; you only have to cross the road and at that time of the day nobody's likely to see you. I'll wait for you with Targhetta in the church and I'll take you to the cell.

GIGLIETTA: Oh, master, whatever are you saying? You want to take a young girl, in this manner, among so many monks? Don't you know what they say? Young girls are not supposed to see a priest except at confession. Wretched me! The abbot will tell the nuns. The nuns spread all the news the moment they hear it, and soon the whole of Pisa will be talking about us. Priests indeed! You also have to consider that the moment they see a girl like this, young and fresh like a rose, they'll think up some way to derive pleasure from it. They'll have you believe that she's possessed and that it will take them two months to exorcise her; that way she'll have to go back to them many times and they'll keep drawing things out.

CASSANDRO: You think that all priests are like the ones you've known. You're wrong. This monk is a holy man. His rooms are secluded and we'll be able to take her to his cell without being seen by anyone.

GIGLIETTA: As you wish. I'd rather surrender my soul than my body to such holy men.

CASSANDRO: You just do as you're told and keep your advice to yourself; go back inside and take Lepida where I told you, the moment you get the chance.

GIGLIETTA: My poor girl, in the hands of priests!

CASSANDRO: Shut up, big mouth, forked tongue. [*Exit Giglietta*] Well it's about time this page boy appeared! [*Enter Targhetta*] What took you so long?

TARGHETTA: A very important matter.

CASSANDRO: Such as what?

TARGHETTA: I drank a bite to eat and ate a glassful[20] because I thought that you were going to send me on a long errand and I didn't want to have to stop right in the middle of it so that I could go home to eat.

CASSANDRO: You certainly look ahead—first you look after yourself and then you think of the others. Come with me.

TARGHETTA: What do you want me to do? Do we need to prepare something for the wedding?

CASSANDRO: There are other matters first. Come with me and hold your tongue; we've to go to the abbot and ask his permission to let these women enter the monastery, and afterwards we'll go into the church through the cloister.
TARGHETTA: Which women, which abbot, master?
CASSANDRO: Come with me and you'll find out. [*Exeunt*]

SCENE VII

MESSER FEDERIGO, a German; CAVICCHIA, his servant

MESSER FEDERIGO: Cavicchia, bring my coat; I'm going out.
CAVICCHIA: [*Upstairs*] Which would you like, sir, the coat or the cloak?
MESSER FEDERIGO: No, I want the overcoat.
CAVICCHIA: [*Upstairs*] If you want eight cloaks,[21] we'll need to borrow some more since there aren't so many in the house.
MESSER FEDERIGO: Just listen to this fool who wants to play with words. I want you to bring me the coat of Neapolitan silk,[22] lined with rough velvet.
CAVICCHIA: [*Upstairs*] Now I understand. I'll bring it straightaway.
MESSER FEDERIGO: [*Aside*] I've certainly found out that mishap begets mishap; as soon as one takes place, you get another and then another. And it's especially true of matters related to the heart.
CAVICCHIA: [*Comes down*] Here's your overcoat, sir, brushed and clean like a mirror.
MESSER FEDERIGO: Put it on. While I'm already distraught by the news that Lepida is married, my suffering is doubled now I hear that, all of a sudden and unexpectedly, she has lost her senses. This is all the more painful to bear since it has befallen such a beautiful and rare creature.
CAVICCHIA: Master, why complain when things have turned out well for you? Had you pursued her with the intention of marrying her, as they do in Germany, you would consider yourself fortunate that, seeing that she has turned out to be mad, she has married somebody else. If you pursue her as your mistress, in the Italian manner,[23] you'll be better off now that she's going mad than you were when she was in control of herself. To tell you the truth, you only get headaches, problems and delays from a woman in

her senses; you're well off only with the crazy ones, for only the mad ones let themselves be plucked.
MESSER FEDERIGO: Just listen to the ravings of this ass![24] Come on, get back inside, make the bed, dust the clothes and tidy up the room. And if Targhetta, the servant in Lepida's house, should come by, tell him that I urgently need to talk to him.
CAVICCHIA: It shall be done. [*Goes upstairs*]
MESSER FEDERIGO: It's odd that Targhetta, who usually reports to me quite diligently what happens in that house, has been out of circulation for the past three days, just when all these important things have been happening. Since I haven't seen him I think I'd better go to the house myself and learn how things are, with the excuse that I need to arrange a lesson with the tutor that lives there. I'd better go there; I feel that I'm about to discover something. Here's the tutor coming this way.

SCENE VIII

MESSER TERENZIO, MESSER FEDERIGO

MESSER TERENZIO: [*Aside*] I've finally sent the letters but I haven't managed to find Lucrezio. I'll go back home since I've been out too long. Here's that bothersome German; he'll certainly want to talk to me. I'll try to get rid of him as soon as I can.
MESSER FEDERIGO: [*Aside*] I must say hullo to him.—Good morning, my good Messer Terenzio; you are a true modern Terence.
MESSER TERENZIO: Greetings to you my second brother.[25] Forgive me, I hadn't seen you as I was lost in my thoughts.
MESSER FEDERIGO: Is that so? Are you busy? Where are you going?
MESSER TERENZIO: Home,[26] to go over the Latin lesson with my young student:[27] nobody who is engaged in the teaching profession can stay away from home too long.
MESSER FEDERIGO: I know. The fact that you are always occupied at home and are never to be seen at the Sapienza[28] or at the schools where all the learned people are, makes me sometimes think of calling on you at home, the way I used to do, so that you can explain to me a passage from Sallust which I couldn't understand last night.
MESSER TERENZIO: Not now,[29] my good Messer Federigo. I'm all absorbed in answering a letter which I received this morning at

dawn³⁰ from the senior tutor of Messer Pierantonio Gambacorta's³¹ children. He wants to test³² the quality of my Ciceronian style. I am confident of success in this challenge. That's all I can say now.

MESSER FEDERIGO: If you'll permit me, I'll come up to your study to read it. That way I shall savour your answer even more.

MESSER TERENZIO: Later. Now my mind is taken up by this composition and I wouldn't want to abort it before having given birth to it.

MESSER FEDERIGO: I didn't think that now—with all the din going on in a household preparing for a wedding—you would have the peace of mind to think.

MESSER TERENZIO: This wedding³³ may never take place.

MESSER FEDERIGO: Why?

MESSER TERENZIO: Because of some trouble which has arisen and which doesn't concern you.³⁴ I must go.

MESSER FEDERIGO: Please, listen to me. What trouble? Is it true what I heard last night about a strange mishap which has befallen the master's daughter?

MESSER TERENZIO: That's enough;³⁵ no more need be said now.³⁶

MESSER FEDERIGO: Listen here, Messer Terenzio, if this wedding will not take place, I'd like to remind you of that favour I mentioned to you the other time.

MESSER TERENZIO: Which one?

MESSER FEDERIGO: In the next university holidays I'd like you to teach me that lesson I requested of you; besides being eternally grateful to you in my thoughts, I'll also be grateful in a way that will be more satisfying to you.

MESSER TERENZIO: Though Fortuna hasn't bestowed on me the gift of riches, I'm easily satisfied.³⁷ Every scholar is rich by virtue of his learning.³⁸ May the mighty³⁹ Jupiter never favour me if I should debase my talent by accepting money⁴⁰ despite the fact that the saying goes: "Every task has its reward"⁴¹ and "the labourer is entitled to his hire."⁴² But I can't satisfy your request now since I'm totally occupied in some pressing matters. Farewell.⁴³

MESSER FEDERIGO: I only want to come up to the study with you for a moment to collect one of Petrarch's works which I happened to leave with you one day.

MESSER TERENZIO: You don't need to come for it now: it won't get lost. But I must entreat you not to leave such books in my house.

If some student of liberal studies should find it in my rooms and think it was mine he'd defame my reputation and my good name.
MESSER FEDERIGO: I beg your pardon? Is there any book which exalts our vulgar language more than Petrarch does?
MESSER TERENZIO: It's called vulgar because it's spoken by the people who know no better. What is this idea of speaking vulgar Italian? We should speak Latin, Latin; Ciceronian, Ciceronian![44]
MESSER FEDERIGO: I'll say this, Messer Terenzio; though I've come to Italy to learn Latin, I must say that in my country Tuscan is highly valued, especially by any person who intends to become a courtier, as is my intention. Indeed it's for this reason that I've come to this university.
MESSER TERENZIO: A courtier! What a heinous crime![45] If you had read and reread as many documents as I have, you'd have found out how the court was first called "morgue."[46] But since men were taken aback by this name, and kept away from the royal rooms, the lords changed the first letter from *m* into *c* and called it "court." But even in this way it still means something evil, as if it shortened men's[47] lives and gave them scanty[48] rewards.
MESSER FEDERIGO: This doesn't scare me at all since, with the intercession of the Archduke of Austria,[49] I hope to enter the service of this prince[50] whose court is an exception to the rule mentioned above.
MESSER TERENZIO: Messer Federigo, don't hold me up any longer. I'll see you tomorrow; don't follow me now.
MESSER FEDERIGO: As you like; I'm in your hands. [*Aside*] I haven't even been able to get into the house to hear some news! My best shot is to hang around here until I come across Targhetta. [*Exit*]
MESSER TERENZIO: [*Aside*] I finally got rid of him. What humiliations a tutor must suffer! How difficult it is for a noble spirit to bear them! We must teach manners to children, put up with the servants' insolence, and satisfy the masters' ignorance—not to mention the fact that each and all want to use you as their lackey! Not only this German but many others, every day, pester me for one thing or another. Even a female servant wanted me to tell her, the other day, what happened to Cain when there was a new moon.[51] But one puts up with these hardships because there is such bliss to be gained. Whatever one says, it's great to be a tutor in a house where there are beautiful ladies. Then why am I loitering around out here? [*Exit*]

ACT II

SCENE I

DRUSILLA, dressed as a pilgrim; RICCIARDO, her companion

RICCIARDO: So now we've seen Pisa cathedral. What a fine building! No wonder it's famous as far away as Spain.
PILGRIM: Yes, it's marvellous! And it shows how important the city must have been in past times.
RICCIARDO: The city's past greatness is witnessed not only by that church, but also by the site and the layout of the city and by all the other buildings. This prince seems to have given it a new lease of life: he's changed it completely from when I saw it last, travelling through as a young man. But since there are no other outstanding sights to be seen in Pisa, we'd better not delay our trip to Loreto. If it's all right with you, my lady, let's set tomorrow for our departure.
PILGRIM: There's no need to hurry now that we're so close to our destination. Given the distance we've already travelled, we can say we're almost there.
RICCIARDO: Were we to stop as long in every city between here and Loreto—and they are no less attractive than this one—we'll never get back to Spain.
PILGRIM: We won't stop this long everywhere.
RICCIARDO: I have the impression that you're attracted to this city and that your eagerness to complete the trip is not as great as it has been so far. When travelling, one should always hurry to get to the destination; then one can undertake the return trip in a more leisurely fashion.
PILGRIM: Four more days cannot make any difference. In the meantime, who knows, Madam Tommasa's health could improve and

she could come with us; that would make things easier. Otherwise we'd have to look for another woman, a total stranger, to go with us.

RICCIARDO: Really, I can't understand why you've changed your mind. Didn't you start making arrangements for us to leave the day before yesterday? As for Madam Tommasa, from what I can see she's so exhausted from the sea voyage that we've already thought of leaving her behind in Pisa since it'll take her too long to recover and set off again with us. Can't you see that she hasn't even been able to come with us on a tour of the city?

PILGRIM: I can see now, Ricciardo, that it's time to confess to you something that I've kept for a happier occasion which, by God's wish, hasn't come about. I know that, since you've raised me, you've always loved me as your daughter; hence I've always revered you as a father. Even if I hadn't given you any proof of this, the fact that I'm entrusting my secret to you will convince you of it.

RICCIARDO: The only reward I've ever wanted for the service I've given to your family is that of proving my loyalty.

PILGRIM: You can believe that if I hadn't been convinced of your loyalty, I wouldn't have chosen you, among all the others my uncle suggested, to keep me company during this trip.

RICCIARDO: I'm certain that's true and I'm proud of it.

PILGRIM: Now, before I say anything else, you must know that this pilgrimage and this vow are only a blind.

RICCIARDO: What's this you're telling me? What's the reason for all this pretence?

PILGRIM: I'll start from the beginning so that you'll understand my constancy and the misfortunes I have endured because of someone else's betrayal. If you think I've been more credulous and bold than I should have been, I beg you to blame my youth and Cupid, who has led more experienced girls than I am into far worse scrapes.

RICCIARDO: I'm startled at such a beginning. Please go on.

PILGRIM: I don't know if you've met a certain Lucrezio Lanfranchi from Pisa, who once stayed in Valencia for two years.

RICCIARDO: I've never met him in person since, as you know, during his stay in Valencia I was in Seville with your uncle on business. But I've heard of him.

PILGRIM: He lived next door to us for a while and, perhaps because

of that, he started showing great interest in me from a very early stage.
RICCIARDO: I'm very disturbed by this news and I'm anxious to learn what the outcome of this story might be.
PILGRIM: I was an inexperienced young girl then, and let my feelings carry me away. I was so attracted by his amorous behaviour, by his exquisite manners. So despite my inner misgivings, I had to admit to myself that I was in love with him. I can't hold anything back from you now, and so I must tell you that he promised to marry me. Since I knew how noble and how well thought of he was by everyone, I accepted him as a husband. As my uncle was not in Valencia, the matter was kept secret between the two of us.
RICCIARDO: Alas, mistress, what are you telling me? What a situation to get yourself into so suddenly and without your elders' permission? Didn't you know how important these things are for a lady's honour?
PILGRIM: Oh don't think that I have, in any way, forsaken my integrity; I call God to witness that I haven't. While we were waiting for my uncle's return hoping that, if he agreed, Lucrezio could give me the ring and marry me publicly, ill-fortune intervened since Lucrezio was called suddenly back to Pisa. But he solemnly promised to return to Valencia within the year at the most.
RICCIARDO: Lovers' promises! You know what they're worth.
PILGRIM: I tell you, the year seemed so long that I thought it would never pass. But even when that year and another six months had passed Lucrezio didn't come back. I felt wretched and, since I had no news of him, I thought about him even more. I passed all my time waiting and pining for him. At times I'd say to myself: Perhaps he's on his way? Perhaps unfavourable winds are delaying him somewhere? Perhaps they've blown him somewhere else? More than once, in the evening, I went to that high loggia which towers over the city so that I could see whether he was coming in the distance; I spent my time in a miserable state torn between distrust and hope, with the former taking, nevertheless, the upper hand. My only reason for hoping was his firm promise, often renewed in his letters. But I was worried by the many reasons which could prevent him from returning.
RICCIARDO: What troubles people are led into by love!
PILGRIM: Meanwhile, since uncle and you had come back, and since I saw that uncle was set on marrying me off, and there had been

other suitors even while he was away, I decided to evade these requests which I couldn't reasonably ignore and to gain time for the return of the only man I wanted and to whom I could possibly belong. For this reason, as you know, I started leading a sheltered, almost hermit-like life and only indulged in prayers, fasts and disciplines.

RICCIARDO: You certainly did astonish us all! Your uncle, who has no one but you, often found himself despairing.

PILGRIM: You must realize that my prayers and abstinences were made with all my heart, in the desire to have Lucrezio back. But when it became clear that the heartless man wasn't returning, my suffering increased, my grief overwhelmed me until I fell into a strange trance. For half a day everyone took me for dead. The whole household started crying and dressing in mourning, and many came to pay their last respects as I was lying on the bier. Had the vital spirits which had abandoned my body remained absent much longer, I would have been taken to church.

RICCIARDO: It was undoubtedly a strange mishap. In the space of a few hours you had us first weeping and then rejoicing.

PILGRIM: How much better it would have been if death had not repented, or if the spell had lasted until I was buried!

RICCIARDO: My lady, my heart goes out to you entirely.

PILGRIM: Though I'd been so close to dying, my original desire didn't diminish. On the contrary, from this accident I derived a reason to hope that I might see Lucrezio again. The moment I felt better, I had uncle and you all believing that I had survived the ordeal because of a vow I'd made to visit the sanctuary of our Virgin Mary of Loreto dressed as a pilgrim. That way I'd get uncle's permission to travel to Italy where I'd perhaps hear and see what had happened to Lucrezio.

RICCIARDO: As it turned out, you organized things with priests and confessors in such a way that you were allowed to leave with me and the most honoured woman in the house as your chosen companions.

PILGRIM: You see how much Love has taught me and how daring it has made me. In the past I only travelled between the nunnery and my house, and when I even heard the sea mentioned I was overawed. Then I became self-assured; I wasn't frightened of such a long and tiring journey, nor did I tremble at the thought of the sea trip.

RICCIARDO: Now I clearly understand not only the reason for your pilgrimage but also for your delay in leaving Pisa. In the four days that you've been here, what have you learnt of Lucrezio?
PILGRIM: I've learnt that I've faithfully loved a man without faith.
RICCIARDO: Why? Has he pretended not to recognize you?
PILGRIM: My intention was not to reveal my identity straightaway but first to find out his present situation. For this reason, the moment we arrived in Italy, I gave out word that I had just arrived from Seville and not from Valencia and had myself called Veronica, not Drusilla. I hoped that this, along with the disguise, would have been enough to prevent him recognising me. And as a further precaution I even asked you to change your name.
RICCIARDO: I was rather surprised at all this and I asked you for an explanation; you told me that you would give it to me at the right time.
PILGRIM: That was my intention. But circumstances have made me do it now.
RICCIARDO: What have you learnt about him?
PILGRIM: The worst I could have learnt about him. That, forgetful of the faith he pledged to me, he has taken a new bride here, only a few days ago. Thus chance has led me here to witness the burial of my love and the funeral of my constancy.
RICCIARDO: If this is the case, why don't we flee this country straightaway, without being seen by such an ungrateful person? If you had known as I do, since I'm Tuscan, the ancient nickname[52] of the Pisan people, you would never have trusted one. Let's go, let's go before he learns of your arrival so that he may not boast that a lady of your standing has travelled all the way from Spain to see him.
PILGRIM: I had already thought of doing this and, as you know, I had arranged to leave the day after we arrived.
RICCIARDO: What has happened to change your mind? Do you intend starting a lawsuit by saying that he had already married you before this other one?
PILGRIM: Absolutely not. I don't want to gain a husband through litigation. But something has happened to revive somewhat the buried hope of having him back.
RICCIARDO: But even if you succeeded, would you take an ungrateful and unfaithful man for a husband? Let's leave him; that's what he deserves. You won't want for loyal husbands who will adore

you.
PILGRIM: I'd rather have this ungrateful and unfaithful husband than a loyal one.
RICCIARDO: What has reawakened your lost hope?
PILGRIM: I've heard from our innkeeper here that the future bride, who lives in the neighbourhood, has been found suffering from some sort of madness and it may very well happen that Lucrezio will reject her. I would, therefore, like to stop here four more days to see the outcome of this matter.
RICCIARDO: Even if that does happen (though the whole thing seems to be an old wives' tale) do you mean to reveal yourself to him so that he may deceive you with his lies a second time?
PILGRIM: If he doesn't get married I'll try to learn his very deepest feelings without revealing myself to him. Since he won't recognize me, it'll be easy for me to do this and I shall decide what to do next according to what I discover. Who knows? Perhaps he's less guilty than we think.
RICCIARDO: I'm very glad you've confided your intention and your plan to me so fully, and I wish you, in this as in every other matter, all that will give you honour and satisfaction. You must make your own decisions in these matters. But now we'd better go in.
PILGRIM: Let's. [*Enter the boarding-house*]

SCENE II

GIGLIETTA, LEPIDA, TARGHETTA

GIGLIETTA: [*In the street*] Come out straight away, Lepida, since there's no one in the street.
LEPIDA: [*Coming out*] How I dread the idea of going to see this monk! You could have tried to talk my father out of his plan!
GIGLIETTA: What did you want me to do? He's so set on finding out whether this malaise is caused by spirits or not that nothing can change his mind. What harm can come to you from seeing this monk? What are you worried about?
LEPIDA: I'm afraid that, in his endeavour to find out whether I'm possessed by some spirit or other, he may realise that I'm not fully in possession of my own.

GIGLIETTA: I thought you were going to say that he might notice what's brewing in your body. You're silly to be frightened. The spirits which are exorcised by priests and friars are of a kind different to yours because those are cursed souls while yours is an angel. Gather your courage and remember my advice: especially while talking to the monk, don't alter the tone of your voice and don't say a word which might be interpreted as one being uttered by a spirit. Otherwise you'll have to go back to that mob time and time again. You only need to act daft and talk nonsense.

LEPIDA: I'll try to do as you say.

GIGLIETTA: And that's exactly the way you have to act in front of your father or anybody else who comes to the house. According to my plan you only need to act out your madness for an hour or two per day; nevertheless, to make it all look real, it's better that you show a certain stupidity in your actions and in your words all the time.

LEPIDA: I'll do my best to follow your instructions, as I have done so far; though it's becoming a great burden.

GIGLIETTA: There are plenty of mad people who try to pass for sane persons, which is much harder! Try to last out until the moment the wedding is called off and the groom leaves. It shouldn't take long. He surely won't spend much time making up his mind whether to marry a madwoman.

LEPIDA: I hope Love will make all these difficulties appear surmountable and all this bother seem like fun.

GIGLIETTA: That's the spirit, child; there's nothing finer in a young girl than being resolute and steadfast when in love. Pull up this dress; it looks as if it's about to fall down. My goodness, you haven't even made yourself up this morning! Look at the mess your hair's in! It's all over the place.

LEPIDA: Well, it's not as if I were going to my wedding! If you ask me, I'm even too presentable. Weren't you saying, not long ago, that I'd do better not to clean myself too much? Isn't it more fitting for a madwoman to appear dishevelled? You're always changing your mind.

GIGLIETTA: That's true, but everything must be done in moderation. If you're looking like a gipsy, I'll get the blame. They'll say: Look at the way she took her out! Even women on their way to the grave are properly made-up and have their hair curled!

LEPIDA: I expect my face will look as if I was coming from the grave!

THE FEMALE PILGRIM

I feel so distressed and destroyed by this groom's visit. How I'd love Messer Terenzio to be here to give me more courage! Everything goes better when the person you love is there.

GIGLIETTA: On the contrary, it's better that he shouldn't be here. It's very difficult to conceal one's passion when you see your loved one suffer.

[*Giglietta busies herself straightening Lepida's dress and hair*]

TARGHETTA: [*Aside*] How true it is that when women have to go somewhere they keep you waiting for a year! It takes them such an effort to tear themselves away from the mirror. That nurse should surely have other things on her mind.

GIGLIETTA: [*Aside to Lepida*] Here's Targhetta coming to hurry us along. Keep your wits about . . . I mean, don't.

TARGHETTA: [*Aside*] Instead of wasting their time with little cream vases, jars and combs, which are worth nothing, how much better they'd spend their time if they attended to cooking-pots, frying-pans and roasting-spits, which are important. All the time spent in their bedrooms could be put to better use in the kitchen. But here they are at last. —Why are you late? My master has been waiting impatiently for you for quite a while now.

GIGLIETTA: Do you expect us to run? It doesn't befit young girls to walk fast. And besides, don't you see how ill she's feeling? Look, look at the way she's acting! Lepida, you heard, we'd better hurry along!

LEPIDA: These are very long trips. Do we have to go along the sea?

TARGHETTA: What do you mean, mistress, along the sea? We're already there.

GIGLIETTA: Please, Targhetta, don't answer her. Can't you see that she isn't making sense? Don't tease her; it'll only make her worse.

LEPIDA: I think I'll have to make this journey in the moonlight.

TARGHETTA: The moon's just right for lunatics!

LEPIDA: Look at that big flock of geese! How beautiful they are! Really beautiful.

TARGHETTA: Where are these geese?

GIGLIETTA: Keep quiet! We've arrived at the church. Let's go in.

LEPIDA: Oh there's a star, ten, a hundred stars! Oh how many suns! Look here, look: a paradise!

GIGLIETTA: Do go in, Lepida. We mustn't keep her out here. Saint Verdiana,[53] help this poor girl! [*Enter the church*]

SCENE III

VIOLANTE, innkeeper; CARLETTO, servant

VIOLANTE: [*Aside*] May all butchers drop dead! As I come into the butchery, I hear: "Violante, come to me for meat, I'll give you a nice little bit." And someone else says: "Take my bit, it hasn't got a bone." And someone else still: "Take this leg and I'll give you the tail with it."[54] Typical! When you're old nobody shows you any respect.

CARLETTO: [*Aside*] If only I can find her at home! She's so often out buying food for her lodgers. But if she isn't in, I'll wait until she gets back. Anyhow, I've nothing else to do.

VIOLANTE: [*Aside*] When I was young and blooming, I had my meat delivered at home; now I have to go and fetch it myself.[55]

CARLETTO: [*Aside*] Here she is, thank God, coming home with her shopping bag. —Good day, my golden honeypot, my little Violante.

VIOLANTE: If I were made of honey, the bees would fly around me more. It's a pity you aren't one of those great scholars; the fact that you show up so rarely would make one think you were.[56]

CARLETTO: Nonsense. You know very well that when someone is employed by others he can't do as he wishes.

VIOLANTE: All the same, you don't have an ounce of love in you. Why is it that I haven't seen you in two whole days? What have I done to you?

CARLETTO: I don't know what you've done to me. I know well what I've come to give you.

VIOLANTE: What?

CARLETTO: A . . .

VIOLANTE: A what? It seems to me you've come to tell a tall tale.

CARLETTO: . . . a message from my master for that pilgrim who's lodging at your house.

VIOLANTE: Is that so, my good Carletto? Now go and tell your master that I'm still too young to take up that profession.[57] Don't you think people are a bit too quick off the mark? The moment a pretty girl arrives in this town, everybody comes running and gets sentimentally amorous.

CARLETTO: Don't be so fussy, Violante. Anyone who works as an innkeeper, as you do, must help fill the clients'[58] beds as well as

their bellies.
VIOLANTE: I was only joking. You know very well I've started carrying out those charitable tasks. I started serving gentlemen when I was twelve. While I was able, I served with actions; now I can see I'll have to start serving with words. But as for this pilgrim, don't count on getting anything out of her.[59] I haven't seen any woman more squeamish and reserved than this one.
CARLETTO: You can't have been around long if you think that. It's exactly these scrupulous women one can rely on. It's better to deal with them. They don't slip through your fingers and they know what they want. It's with them that the men really get down to business.
VIOLANTE: That's the way you see it. I don't, and I think I know this type of business pretty well. The moment she set foot in my house, I guessed that she was one of those for just the reason you give. I thought I was onto a good thing. But instead she turned out to be strong-willed and unmalleable; I lost all hopes.
CARLETTO: You've given up too soon. She's a woman who gads about and she's Spanish. There's no more to add.
VIOLANTE: Just remember that anyone who knows the profession as I do, only needs to talk twice to a woman to know if she'll do or not. This woman will never have anything to do with men. It's not her nature.
CARLETTO: And I thought that such a woman couldn't exist!
VIOLANTE: I'll tell you Carletto. Sometimes you can see in someone certain oddities that you don't see in a thousand persons. Don't we know that for some people roses stink, that others don't like rock melons and similar things? Once in a hundred years a woman is born who's so cold and insensitive that she isn't at all interested in love. Is there anything worse? And it's my bad luck and your master's that this pilgrim is one such woman.
CARLETTO: As she pleases. Well, that's her business. Anyway, to tell you the truth, this has nothing to do with what my master wants.
VIOLANTE: What does he want then?
CARLETTO: He's heard, and I've confirmed it since I've heard it from you, that this pilgrim knows many things and gains everybody's admiration. Since his bride went half mad two or three days ago, he'd like to come and ask her advice. Do you think she might help him out?
VIOLANTE: We were talking about Lepida's misfortune only the other

night. I assure you my pilgrim knows all about it because she wanted to know all the details; she is just what your master wants. She's kindly disposed towards other women and she'll be happy to help this poor girl. If it had been a man, it would have been otherwise since she calls all men cheats and betrayers.

CARLETTO: Well then, I'll tell my master he can come and talk with her.

VIOLANTE: Tell him to come when he wants. And don't forget me.

CARLETTO: How do you expect me to forget you when I've always thought of you as a mother?

VIOLANTE: Like a mother, indeed! May you get an abscess! Like a mother-in-law, you should have said.

CARLETTO: Why mother-in-law?

VIOLANTE: Because mothers-in-law give away their own flesh and blood and their possessions.

CARLETTO: Yes I understand, my little Violante. You're referring to the two scudi you lent me. Don't worry, the moment I get my wages I'll pay you back. Perhaps this evening, as soon as the master's bedded down for the night and your guests are asleep, I'll come and pay over two or three instalments.

VIOLANTE: Don't tell me lies and don't keep me waiting. You know, I've kept a flask of muscatel for you which would resuscitate the dead.

CARLETTO: We'll perform the service for the dead and the living, don't worry.[60] Be seeing you. [*Exit*]

VIOLANTE: I must get back inside. This fellow has made me waste enough time out here. [*Enters the boarding-house*]

SCENE IV

MESSER TERENZIO, CASSANDRO

MESSER TERENZIO: [*Aside*] There's no way I can bear to stay at home now Lepida's gone out. I'd like to go to this monastery. That way I'll be near her and at the same time I'll make her father think I'm concerned for her. How sorry I feel for such a young girl who, out of love for me, doesn't worry about being thought to be mad or about submitting herself to such torments. When will I be able to repay such an obligation? But here's the old man coming out of the church.

CASSANDRO: [*Aside*] We must think of a new plan; the monk says it's certainly not a case of spirits. —Where are you going tutor?
MESSER TERENZIO: Oh my lord,[61] greetings. As I'm worried for you in this difficult time, I was coming to see how things were[62] and if I could be of any help.[63]
CASSANDRO: Things are not too good. I had hoped that this was a case of spirits and I was sure that, if that was so, Don Marcello would have exorcised her immediately. Now we have to consider that there's another cause for this illness.
MESSER TERENZIO: I always thought it was useless to take her to this monk.
CASSANDRO: Enough, I wanted to satisfy myself. What upsets me is that now I've little hope of seeing her cured. Wretched me! What consolations does my old age hold for me?
MESSER TERENZIO: Don't despair, my lord: "[The well prepared spirit] hopes in times of adversity and fears in times of prosperity,"[64] et cetera. It must have been a melancholic temperament which dulled the cerebrum, as happens sometimes, because of an unforeseen mental derangement.
CASSANDRO: Where could she get this melancholic humour?[65] She has a very sanguine nature. And as for the worries, she had no reason to have any since I've always mollycoddled her and never reprimanded her even by a look.
MESSER TERENZIO: Very sensible.[66] As that character of Terence's, Micione, says:"[It's always best to try and control] our children by care and benevolence" . . . and what follows.[67]
CASSANDRO: I think it must be my sins that are being punished. As for her, she's as pure as a dove. Apart from a few close relatives, she hasn't known any other man but you.
MESSER TERENZIO: And how sensibly she behaves with me! You can really pride yourself on having generated a second Penelope. I appreciate the nature of this young girl more every day.[68]
CASSANDRO: She had all the things that a young girl can wish for; all she needed to be fully contented was a husband. And now she has that too.
MESSER TERENZIO: Perhaps[69] that's the cause of her strange derangement. Sometimes the bashfulness of these young girls is such that the unaccustomed familiarity with a man throws them into a panic which produces these effects.
CASSANDRO: I want to try all possible ways to cure her and, before I

place her in the hands of our doctor, I've decided to find out what a female pilgrim, who has been mentioned to me, can do for her.

MESSER TERENZIO: Don't go to her. She's bound to be some poisonous female quack.[70]

CASSANDRO: I've heard great things about her. When this morning I was describing my daughter's illness to our Burgundian neighbour, he told me that in Violante's inn there's this Spanish pilgrim who, in the four days she's been in Pisa, has already performed miracles. He especially recounted how one of Violante's neighbours had been in the throes of labour for three days and had been declared a goner; well, the first day this pilgrim arrived, having heard this, she went to see her and told her immediately that she had nothing to fear because she was about to give birth to twins. After she'd whispered only a few words in her ear, everything happened as predicted.

MESSER TERENZIO: But this isn't a case of giving birth to a child: Lepida hasn't yet had carnal knowledge of a man.[71]

CASSANDRO: True, but I'm telling you this to give you proof of the excellent quality of this woman. Listen to this other story. A weaver, here in the neighbourhood, had suffered so much after childbirth for eight uninterrupted days that she was given for dead. This pilgrim cured her with some oil of hers in just over an hour.

MESSER TERENZIO: Careful, careful![72] This must be a witch and Violante is circulating this story to attract clients to her establishment. I know from my reading that one must not trust a vagabond woman.

CASSANDRO: She's noble by birth, from what they say. She's accompanied by respectable people and is going to Loreto to fulfill a vow.

MESSER TERENZIO: All the more reason[73] to be wary of appearances. They want to appear beautiful to everyone[74] to dupe the simpletons more easily. Spanish trickery!

CASSANDRO: She's young and she can't have any such wickedness in her.

MESSER TERENZIO: Young people are without the experience which is above all[75] desirable in those who peddle such arcane remedies. Why do you think that the ancients painted Aesculapius[76] with a long beard if not to show that the good doctor must be of a certain age?

CASSANDRO: I saw this pilgrim yesterday and I liked her very much.

I've decided to place Lepida in her hands. What harm can come of it?

MESSER TERENZIO: There could be great harm since theory without practice is misleading.[77] Furthermore[78] every kind of medication can cause a disease. Let nature run its course. That way less will be heard of the whole matter. Believe me, I'm driven to say these things out of love.

CASSANDRO: I know you mean well, but I can't let her put up with this suffering any longer. I'm well disposed towards this woman. I mean to go and talk to her the moment I've found Lucrezio. I want to tell him of the outcome of our visit to the monk and also of this intention of mine. I'll also try to sweeten him and keep him from doing anything rash. [*Exit*]

MESSER TERENZIO: All the best.[79] I'll go back home since I've to give Rutilio his test. [*Aside*] Poor me! It now seems that chance has sent us this pilgrim to cause our downfall; she's Spanish and, therefore, shrewd and wise. She's a vagabond woman, a quack doctor. She'll notice immediately that the sickness is feigned and, what's worse, she may discover the pregnancy. And that would really be the end. Alas, in what a tempestuous sea our ship is travelling; no sooner has it avoided one reef than it strikes another! [*Exit*]

SCENE V

MESSER FEDERIGO, TARGHETTA

MESSER FEDERIGO: [*Aside*] This Targhetta's like the quintessence[80] of the alchemists: he's never to be found. Where can he have gone? Amongst the misfortunes of people in love this is the worst: to be at the mercy of reckless and indiscreet people.

TARGHETTA: [*Aside*] I'm sure glad I didn't die last night, because I'd have missed out on all the adventures I've had this morning in this monastery.

MESSER FEDERIGO: [*Aside*] Aren't I tolerant with him? Don't I pay him properly?

TARGHETTA: [*Aside*] But here's the German. He'll certainly give me my share of 'adventures' since I didn't tell him anything about the mistress's madness. I'll find some excuse. It's easy to fool people in love.

MESSER FEDERIGO: [*Aside*] Here he is, thank God. —It's not easy to get a sight of you, Targhetta. You've been keeping yourself out of the way.
TARGHETTA: Don't complain, master Federigo. I do more for you when you don't see me than when I'm with you. I know that what you especially want me to do is to get you into Lepida's good books. Isn't it true that I can do that better if I'm near her rather than you?
MESSER FEDERIGO: That's true. But you should still keep me informed day by day, and especially when important things are happening, as they have been lately.
TARGHETTA: Do you mean this disease that's been troubling the mistress in the past two days?
MESSER FEDERIGO: Exactly. Do you think it's something unimportant?
TARGHETTA: I've been so busy because of it that I've hardly been able to leave home and I didn't want to burden you with this until I could give you the bad and the good news together.
MESSER FEDERIGO: What is the good news?
TARGHETTA: I had a feeling the bridegroom wanted to reject her and I knew nothing would please you more than to hear that this marriage arrangement has been broken off.
MESSER FEDERIGO: I certainly would have liked to hear this if it had been for any another reason. But since this misfortune has befallen the woman I adore, this news saddens me more than the news about the wedding.
TARGHETTA: Cheer up! This sickness will soon disappear, I can feel it. Well, here it is: the master feared it might be a case of spirits but now it has been ascertained and verified by a monk who understands these things that it isn't so. They sent Lepida to consult him at the monastery nearby. Ha! Ha! Ha!
MESSER FEDERIGO: What are you laughing about? Is this a thing to joke about?
TARGHETTA: I'm laughing because of a joke I played on one of those monks; I'd like to tell you about it.
MESSER FEDERIGO: I'm not interested in your jokes.
TARGHETTA: I want you to hear it. You must know that as the mistress entered Don Marcello's cell—that's the name of the monk who knows about spirits—there he was sitting in a chair like a pope. He could only move his hands, which he used to give some sort of blessing. Then, a whole lot of younger monks started coming

in one after the other, until the room was chock-a-block, and with great joy and excitement they made a circle round the poor girl. There were some hefty young friars with cheeks as red as dawn and they couldn't stay still.

MESSER FEDERIGO: Really! And what did Lepida do?

TARGHETTA: She stood there looking like a poor lost lamb. After a while, she looked as if she was going to faint. The monks buzzed around like wasps. Some ran for rose-scented water to sprinkle her face, others fetched vinegar and tried to rub her wrists. One young chap (more heated with the spirit of charity than the others) went for her buckles with the intention of unfastening them. The nurse was huffing and puffing, hovering about and keeping them at bay by applying the rose-scented water and vinegar herself. I'm certain that if my master hadn't been there she wouldn't have gone back home in one piece.

MESSER FEDERIGO: Please, say no more; I can't stand it.

TARGHETTA: But I haven't yet told you of my trick. You must remember that those monks who had run to see this novelty in their monastery had almost all left their cells open in the hurry. I had noticed this, and seeing that they were interested in the proceedings I thought they were bound to stay until the end. So I started going into the cells. I found one, among others, which was beautifully done up, and full of luxury items. There was a beautiful crystal mirror, and a little velvet hat embroidered in gold. In a small wardrobe I found hundreds of pretty little things, and a number of jars filled with perfumed waters.[81] There were a couple of finely-knitted garments and many other knick-knacks worthy of such friars: breviaries, paternoster beads and whips, the whole works. Out of caution I only took a beautiful container which was guilded in the French style—the most charming thing you've ever seen.

MESSER FEDERIGO: No reform can have yet entered this cell. Did you rob a monk then?

TARGHETTA: Rob? I wanted to do a charitable work by relieving him of some superfluities and of the chance to fall prey to lust.

MESSER FEDERIGO: Do you intend to keep what you acquired with deceit?

TARGHETTA: No sir; I've decided to give it as a present to a deserving girl for the soul of a friend of mine.

MESSER FEDERIGO: Admirable intention. What do you think? Do you think that friars are so insensitive that they don't enjoy beautiful things?

TARGHETTA: I think they do enjoy beautiful and nice things and, to show how true this is, I ran afterwards into the cellarman who comes from my village and who took me to the cellar where I tasted a holy wine. To conclude, rich friars enjoy their paradise in this world and in the other one.

MESSER FEDERIGO: Come on, forget about these things; give me some details of this mishap which has befallen my lady Lepida. What illness has she? How does it affect her?

TARGHETTA: It's not very clear what she has. She's always looking dull-witted and stunned; she turns her head this way and that, mutters a few things which don't make sense, and won't let anyone near her.

MESSER FEDERIGO: Good Lord, what a strange thing! What a sad misfortune!

TARGHETTA: Do you want me to say what I really think?

MESSER FEDERIGO: Yes, go ahead.

TARGHETTA: I'm afraid that you may be the cause of this illness.

MESSER FEDERIGO: How could I cause any illness to the woman to whom I want to give all my love? In what way? What have I done?

TARGHETTA: She loved you so much and was so set on having you for her husband; and the fact that she was betrothed to this other man, I think, must have caused her to lose her wits out of despair. And you'll see that, if the marriage doesn't take place, (as I think will be the case), she'll get over this trouble and this illness; then you'll have twice as much reason to rejoice.

MESSER FEDERIGO: God grant that you're right, Targhetta. If you are, you won't lose by it.

TARGHETTA: I feel sure that it's so. And within three days I'll be able to let you know something definite.

MESSER FEDERIGO: Make sure you come and see me every day, whatever happens.

TARGHETTA: Certainly I will, since that's what you want. I'm so much indebted to you!

MESSER FEDERIGO: What I've done so far is nothing in comparison to what I shall do.

TARGHETTA: Thank you. Please go now—but I'll always be thinking of you! Listen, if you want to see Lepida, go that way towards the monastery because you'll either meet her in the street or find her in church.

MESSER FEDERIGO: I'm glad you told me. I'll go to the church and from there I'll get to my room through the other door by going down the alley. [*Exit*]

TARGHETTA: Off you go now. [*Aside*] These Germans! When they're in love they're always gullible and will always be duped by Italians. I don't remember how long ago I ran into this chap who was pining away for my mistress; he started taking me to his house, offering me drinks and giving me a gift now and then if I did some little errand for him. Since I thought I had found a real simpleton, I tried to see how Lepida felt about him; but she wasn't at all interested in men and she didn't like him at all. I could see I wouldn't get much by telling the truth so I decided to resort to lies. As far as I'm concerned, anything goes as long as the money comes in. . . . How nicely I've kept him dangling, with a lie here and there! Sometimes he sent her a short letter and, after the third one, I answered with feminine words which were, like good wine, bitter and sweet at the same time. And do you know how well it worked? Not even three days passed before he brought me a beautiful necklace so that I could give it on his behalf to Madam Lepida. But instead it ended up in my purse. It's true though, that I showed it to Lepida. I told her it belonged to a friend who wanted to sell it and, since she liked it, she asked me if she could keep it for two days. While she was wearing it, I made an excuse to get her to show herself at the window just when this German was passing by. As he recognized the necklace, he considered it a great honour that the young girl had shown herself while wearing it. So he doubled my tip! In this way, between my cleverness and his stupidity, things have gone well for me and if this illness doesn't ruin everything, I can carry on like this for a while. What a lot of dirty tricks maids and servants can play on these poor infatuated lovers who have to rely on other people! [*Exit*]

SCENE VI

LEPIDA, GIGLIETTA [nurse][82]

LEPIDA: I'm afraid, nurse, that we've stayed too long in this chapel and that father will be upset.

GIGLIETTA: I wanted to wait until everybody left the church so that you weren't seen, but that nuisance of a German was playing his tricks again. I think he'd have paced up and down that church all day long if we hadn't gone.
LEPIDA: If he only knew how much I dislike him, he wouldn't even come near me.
GIGLIETTA: Come on, Lepida, women always like to see their admirers.
LEPIDA: That's not what I'd say. But what do you think, nurse? Did I bear myself well? Haven't I been good at pretending to be crazy?[83]
GIGLIETTA: Very good indeed, dear child. Your actions, your words, your blunders were well chosen.[84] I tell you, I was almost convinced that you had really gone mad. Well, that's that; you did so well that we shouldn't have to come back here again.
LEPIDA: Come back? I don't know whether I could. Those tiresome friars annoyed me so much!
GIGLIETTA: I think you've charmed them.
LEPIDA: Thank God we got out of there in one piece. But what will my Lucrezio say now? Will he say I love him or not?
GIGLIETTA: He didn't need this test to confirm it. But listen to what I'm saying: there aren't many women around who could be as faithful as you are, and who would have faced so many dangers for love. Most women like attention, but they live very much in the present. If there's any trouble, if a chance is lost, if a lover has to go far away, they forget it after a day, they shake their heads and hang on to those they can or to those who stick around; and it's too bad for whoever is unavailable or isn't on the spot.
LEPIDA: Women who behave like this can't be noble of heart. A generous heart must be certain before surrendering to someone; but when it has come to a worthy decision then, no matter what happens, such a heart must persevere to the end.
GIGLIETTA: Eh, Lepida, that was in the good old days when a certain etiquette was still observed;[85] in those days any woman who entertained more than one lover would have been considered a flirt. But today things have changed. A woman who doesn't have a number of lovers doesn't feel important enough. She demands a knight to go to tournaments and jousts, a rich man to give gifts, a musician to serenade her, a lowly one for odd jobs; one to entertain them in the country, another in the city and, finally, a learned one to compose sonnets and songs.

LEPIDA: Other women can do what they like. I've chosen one. I only want him and he's enough for me.
GIGLIETTA: That's the way, child; that's the way wise women behave. I just wanted to hear you say it.
LEPIDA: That's enough then. I hope I'll always cherish him and be happy with him. [Cassandro][86] can't deny me that; in the meantime the documents from my Lucrezio's country are on the way. Oh how happy life will be, nurse, if they arrive!
GIGLIETTA: May God bestow his graces upon us! Now let's go in. We'll have time to talk later on.
LEPIDA: Yes, let's go. It seems that I've had to wait a thousand years to tell the outcome[87] to my sweet Lucrezio who is waiting. [*Enter the house*]

SCENE VII

LUCREZIO, RICCIARDO, PILGRIM

LUCREZIO: [*Aside; in the street*] I want to satisfy myself, with the help of this pilgrim, whether I've been duped or not. Two or three of my relatives have spoken to me and are surprised that I'm not taking offence at all this; they're advising me not to go ahead with it. Alas! If she'd been lame or blind in one eye I could have put up with it; but mad! Since Carletto's told me I can go and talk to her whenever I feel like it, I'd better hurry. —Anybody home?
RICCIARDO: [*Inside*] Who's down there?
LUCREZIO: Is that Spanish pilgrim at home?
RICCIARDO: [*Aside*] This must be Lucrezio. May God help me. —Is your Lordship perhaps the same gentleman who sent his servant to Violante not long ago?
LUCREZIO: Yes, sir; it's I.
RICCIARDO: [*Aside*] I'm not happy with this but she wants to talk to him.
LUCREZIO: What are you saying?
RICCIARDO: I'm saying that your Lordship can talk to her. Please wait a little while and she'll come down.
LUCREZIO: I'll wait; tell her to come when she's ready. [*Aside*] How I'd like to free myself from this marriage, to find out that this illness is either an old one or an incurable one. Then all I'd need

to do would be to give back to Cassandro the thousand scudi I received on signing the marriage contract.

PILGRIM: [*Comes outside*] What does your Lordship wish?

LUCREZIO: I had come to ask you a favour, but now your presence makes me afraid and I've almost changed my mind.

PILGRIM: What do you fear, sir? Do you change your mind so quickly?

LUCREZIO: Your noble aspect makes me hold back. I fear you might think that I want to avail myself of your services in a matter which is too low and unbecoming for you.

PILGRIM: Among noble spirits one finds only discretion in asking and promptness in giving; so, you can rest assured that you will be granted what you ask.

LUCREZIO: I'll talk freely then since I'm so disposed by the kindness of your heart. I've heard that in the few days since your arrival in Pisa you've carried out some miraculous cures. Your noble presence makes me believe that you aren't doing this as a profession; nevertheless, I know it's not unbefitting for noble people to possess such secret powers and to be generous with others either out of charity or out of kindness.

PILGRIM: I've indeed a few secrets which I inherited; they've been passed down for a long time from father to son. But I don't profess in any way to be a doctor. It is true that while staying here in these lodgings I have used these medications to the benefit of two ladies in the region, and I would as willingly offer them to you as well. But I marvel that the news of them has spread so quickly.

LUCREZIO: I'm very grateful to you. I should explain, then, that I took a bride a few days ago and even before I went to see her she was found to give signs of madness; at times she says and does strange things.

PILGRIM: This is truly a pitiful case, especially since you must have loved this young girl beforehand.

LUCREZIO: Not at all. I only decided to marry her because of pressures placed on me by my family.

PILGRIM: You must have at least started loving her after becoming betrothed to her.

LUCREZIO: No, I've only visited her twice.

PILGRIM: Have you given her the ring?

LUCREZIO: Not yet, and that at least is a consolation. Otherwise I'd really be desperate. But since I'm not yet committed, I want to

understand the nature of this illness fully.
PILGRIM: Should this be a desperate case, do you intend breaking off the marriage agreement?
LUCREZIO: The nobility of your bearing makes me talk freely. My inclination, madam, whatever the situation is, is *not* to take this wife.
PILGRIM: If that's how you feel, why do you want me to visit her?
LUCREZIO: I want to get an expert opinion so that I can have a more plausible excuse to offer her father, since I think the matter is as I suspected.
PILGRIM: This decision of yours is certainly wise. I think you're quite right not to want to go ahead with this marriage, since one never is entirely cured of such humours, and it can be argued that such women will bear children who will suffer from the same condition. Besides the misfortune of having such a wife in the house there is also a certain amount of shame.
LUCREZIO: You're confirming what I thought. But I'm trying to act without hurting her father and those who have compelled me to enter this marriage.
PILGRIM: Why compelled you? Wasn't the young woman suitable to your status?
LUCREZIO: Suitable, yes. But taking a wife shouldn't be like some business deal where one must accept only what is available in place of what he truly desires. If a man can't have the wife he wants, then he shouldn't have one at all.
PILGRIM: I'm surprised that in this city someone like you, first among the nobles, has been refused by a woman. What was the obstacle?
LUCREZIO: My lady, you can't be interested in my personal affairs and it is extremely painful for me to bring certain things back to memory either here or anywhere. That's enough. My plans have been thwarted and there's no more remedy.
PILGRIM: [*Aside*] Alas! Don't you think I was deeply hurt too?
LUCREZIO: What were you saying, madam?
PILGRIM: I say that fortune has indeed hurt you a lot.
LUCREZIO: Truly said! And not satisfied yet, it has schemed to place this new burden on me.
PILGRIM: You're not the only one to experience the cruelty of fortune: I too am its victim. I had just married a man of my heart and an unfair destiny has deprived me of him. It's because of this that I've embarked upon such a long pilgrimage. I've stopped here to

search for someone very dear and precious to me. But, as far as I can make out, I'm on the wrong track.

LUCREZIO: Please let me know if I can be of any help in your search; I wish nothing better than to place myself at your service.

PILGRIM: You could have helped a lot, but now I've found that my task is hopeless; there's no solution left any longer.

LUCREZIO: I'm very sorry to hear it: I wanted the chance to show you what kind of man I am.

PILGRIM: I know what kind of man you are without you having to give any proof of it.

RICCIARDO: [*Aside*] I'm afraid that either he'll recognize her or she'll reveal herself to him. [*To the pilgrim*] Madam, you'd better hurry because something's happened to your maid.

PILGRIM: I'm coming. Sir, I must leave you. When you think it's time for me to see your bride, let me know and I won't let you down.

LUCREZIO: I'll fix a time with her father and let you know; your countenance assures me that you don't say things just to please someone.

PILGRIM: Rest assured that I'm yours to command, and yours only.

LUCREZIO: Let me kiss your hands, your Ladyship. And to tell you the truth, I don't know how to part from you; I so much enjoy hearing you speak Italian so well. Were you perhaps raised in Italy?

PILGRIM: No, sir; but I've learnt the language from a good Tuscan teacher.

LUCREZIO: Happy days!

PILGRIM: A woman as unfortunate as I am can hardly be happy.

LUCREZIO: [*Aside*] Speaking to this woman makes me happy and sad at the same time. It's because, in her accents and her looks, she reminds me of my blessed Drusilla. [*Exit*]

PILGRIM: [*Aside*] Dear God, have I changed so much from what I used to be or has this dress transfigured me to such an extent that Lucrezio hasn't recognized me? But it's you who are changed, Lucrezio; you've directed your feelings elsewhere, and now you don't even recognize your Drusilla. Is it possible that neither the face nor the gestures nor the words have reminded you of her?

RICCIARDO: [*Now outside*] I think, madam, you'd have spoken to him all day long if I hadn't separated you with the excuse of Tommasa.

PILGRIM: You've interrupted my few moments of consolation. Didn't

I tell you how I wanted to behave towards him? What were you worried about?
RICCIARDO: I was afraid his presence and his words would have made you change your mind. You wouldn't be the first woman who, having set out to talk to her lover with a particular purpose, changed her mind in his presence.
PILGRIM: To be honest, after his words betrayed his ungratefulness, I nearly revealed myself and threw it in his face. But I restrained myself because I gathered that he wants to reject this wife at all costs. Since he wants something from me, I'll be able to use that to learn more of his most intimate thoughts—beyond the obvious fact that he seems to love somebody else.
RICCIARDO: Why, then, do you call him ungrateful?
PILGRIM: Because he said that he's been thwarted in his plans to win a bride he desired.
RICCIARDO: Those words could just as well have referred to you as to somebody else. What do you know of the obstacles he could have had? A person in love always takes things in their negative sense.
PILGRIM: I must admit that I haven't given up all hope. I'll need to talk to him once more so as to get to know everything. But so far I think I've more to fear than to hope.
RICCIARDO: I can't wait for the moment when the whole business will be cleared up. What remedy can you suggest for his bride's illness?
PILGRIM: I'll tell you everything inside.
RICCIARDO: And people say that chance isn't all powerful! Two secret remedies that you've used by chance in this city have given you the reputation of a soothsayer and a great doctor. There must be many people who acquire reputation and fame, out of sheer luck, in matters of which they're completely ignorant.
PILGRIM: You're not saying what is most important. Chance has brought about a situation in which my lover needs my skill. If I can prove for him that the illness is incurable and dates back to the past, I can have some hope that he'll reject her.
RICCIARDO: Tell me, please, how do you intend to manage that?
PILGRIM: I'll tell you inside, at our leisure. Let's go in. It must be time for lunch. [*Enter the boarding-house*]

ACT III

SCENE I

GIGLIETTA, MESSER TERENZIO

GIGLIETTA: Leave it to me, Messer Terenzio; I know what has to be done.
MESSER TERENZIO: If she isn't at home, wait for her; we absolutely have to talk to her before the old man does.
GIGLIETTA: I'll keep my eyes open, don't worry. The things one must keep an eye on to carry off this deceit!
MESSER TERENZIO: Listen, Giglietta, one more thing. Oh dear, we haven't thought of something which could prejudice the whole thing.
GIGLIETTA: What?
MESSER TERENZIO: If it's better to reveal Lepida's pregnancy; since this pilgrim is such a knowledgeable woman, she might notice it and reveal it unintentionally.
GIGLIETTA: That's true; it could easily be our downfall. We'd better tell her.
MESSER TERENZIO: I'm not sure what to do. It might not be a good idea to let her know so much. Don't tell her anything unless you have to. You'll soon find out what sort of woman she is; since we have to win her over, give and promise as you see fit and don't come away without having won her support.
GIGLIETTA: If this is a woman who can be bought, I have what it takes; if she acts out of kindness then she won't want to be the cause of a young girl's ruin.
MESSER TERENZIO: Go, now. [*Exit*]
GIGLIETTA: [*Aside*] The risk we're taking is a big one but we've good reason for taking it. I won't say anything to Violante yet, though.

She's my friend and we've been involved in a few things together, but I wouldn't trust her with a secret like this one; in the end it's always us women who let out one another's secrets and get one another into scrapes. [*Outside the boarding house*] But there's no one here. I'll have to call. —Hey, Violante, Violante.

SCENE II

VIOLANTE, GIGLIETTA

VIOLANTE: [*Inside*] Who's there? Who's calling me?
GIGLIETTA: A friend. Come down here a moment.
VIOLANTE: First I must put this load of washing in the tub so I don't ruin the clothes, and then I have to clean myself up.
GIGLIETTA: Come as you are, for goodness' sake. I'm in a hurry, and anyway, there's no one here who'll mind if you aren't dressed properly. [*Aside*] She must be in the middle of her washing. I see smoke in the house and I can hear the hot water being let out of the tub.
VIOLANTE: Oh it's you, you old nuisance![88] See how you've made me come down.
GIGLIETTA: It doesn't matter, it's only me. I guessed you were doing the washing! I must say, you don't look too bad done up like this. Look at those huge arms!
VIOLANTE: I'm not sure, Giglietta. One must keep one's flab tucked away as much as possible. It's no good letting it all hang out when it's old and withered. But what about you? What are you up to?
GIGLIETTA: I've come to have a word with the pilgrim staying in your house.
VIOLANTE: Ho, ho, people are starting to pour in. My boarding house will become well known. You watch. You must have come to bring her a message. But I hope you haven't come to lure away my clients. Have you?
GIGLIETTA: Really, how can you say that? I wouldn't try to compete with you in your profession. I wanted to speak to her because, as I understand, she is very knowledgeable about many things.
VIOLANTE: Now I get it, you want her to reveal some of her secrets to you. Perhaps you need to help some young girl or some poor widow?

GIGLIETTA: If that was what I needed, I'd have come to you. After all, you're good at those things and I wouldn't want to offend you.
VIOLANTE: Get away![89] Me good? When I wanted my Sandrino to travel forty miles to come and see me whenever I felt like it, who taught me that spell done with a thrust of a knife? Wasn't it you?
GIGLIETTA: What about the time I wanted to seek revenge against my lover who was trying to hide away with his whore all the time? Who taught me then how to cool his passion and freeze his lust so that he didn't get it up for three whole months? Let's stop this and let's not quarrel. I've come to see if she wants to give my master some professional help. He's in a spot of bother.
VIOLANTE: I get you; it's about that young girl, isn't it? You don't need to worry about that. The groom was here not long ago.
GIGLIETTA: The groom has been here?
VIOLANTE: Yes, and he talked with her for quite a while.
GIGLIETTA: Anyhow, I still want to have a little talk with her. After all, as you know, there are certain details of a woman's condition that men can't describe or understand.
VIOLANTE: Come up and I'll take you to her room. Then I'll go and add some more ash and boil another copperful. Meanwhile you can talk to her at leisure. You'll soon see she's a truly kind person.
GIGLIETTA: Lead the way.
VIOLANTE: Do you know, Giglietta, what I'd like you to do since you know a thing or two? Try to study her and see what you think of her. It's a shame that she should leave without meeting some nice gentleman or other. I haven't dared suggest it yet; she seems too saintly.
GIGLIETTA: I never thought you'd be scared to try something like that. I thought you were an old hand in your profession and, instead, you turn out to be a rookie. Don't you know that women are like birds? They can all be caught in the end if you use the right approach. Vain women are captured with flattery, miserly women with gifts, haughty women by kissing their feet and simple women with cajolery. Leave it to me, I'll know exactly what she's worth after I've looked her over. [*Enter the boarding house*]

SCENE III

TARGHETTA, VIOLANTE

TARGHETTA: [*Aside*] Just look at the useless gifts I'm collecting today! I just met Sandra at the corner. With a nice curtsy, she gave me a bunch of flowers and said: "Smell this, if you love me." As soon as she was out of sight I threw it away. I don't feed on the scent of flowers! If I weren't embarassed, I wouldn't want to carry anything around but the cork of a bottle which had had good wine in it. I'd sniff that at every step!
VIOLANTE: [*Downstairs*] Now that I've taken her to the pilgrim's room, I'll shut the door so that nobody will come and disturb them.
TARGHETTA: [*Aside*] Since I've taken my master's message, I'd better go and tell him the reply; but before I go home I'll just see if he's at Violante's where he said he'd be. But here's Violante at the door. She'll tell me if she's seen him. —Hey, milady, why are you closing the door?
VIOLANTE: Because it's necessary when there are bad characters about. Tell me what you want quickly; I'm in a hurry. I've left the copper for the washing boiling on the fire and I don't want it to boil over.
TARGHETTA: Well, since you're doing the washing, why don't you wash some rags of mine?
VIOLANTE: I'll tell you why. I don't put any rags in my washing; why should I take yours?
TARGHETTA: Come on, Violante, a pair of trousers and a pair of underpants. What sort of talk is that? You certainly must have put somebody else's trousers in.
VIOLANTE: Yes I have, and yours would fit in too. But those other pants belong to my guests and to people who don't have anyone to do their washing; you can go and get your pants cleaned by your fancy women in the house where you dirtied them. What's the real reason you called in?
TARGHETTA: I wanted to know if my master came to talk to the pilgrim who's staying in your house.
VIOLANTE: Targhetta, he hasn't been. [*Aside*] This man has come to worm out some information on Giglietta. You won't learn anything about her, upon my word you won't.
TARGHETTA: What are you saying?

VIOLANTE: Upon my word, you won't make it with the pilgrim; she's not made for old men or people like you.

TARGHETTA: [*Aside*] I think I'll pull her leg a bit. —Violante, to tell you the truth, I came to you because you do works of charity like putting up pilgrims, feeding the hungry and helping the needy. I thought you might do me the favour of finding a wet-nurse for the baby of a friend of mine.

VIOLANTE: I see; I'll do my best. Are you looking for a young girl who hasn't given milk before?

TARGHETTA: No, no, I'd settle for a woman who's done it already. These young ones don't know how to get themselves used to the job: they have to be taught everything from scratch. As well as having a bit of experience I'd like her to be youngish, cheery, a bit saucy, and able to look after a delicate child. It's a white child, as long as an arm.

VIOLANTE: I think I know someone who'll be just right for you. Someone with huge breasts, you know! She's got so much milk she could feed four babies a day. The moment she starts to like the child, I promise she'll fall in love with it; she'll make it grow as big as a long hardened stick. But you must be prepared to keep her at home, right?

TARGHETTA: No fear; it's too much trouble to raise kids and keep nurses at home. I'd want her to stay at her place, but I'd pay her, give her white bread for the pap, pay her lots of little courtesies and form a lifelong friendship. Oh, I've got something here that I want to put in her hand the moment I see her. Look, here it is.

VIOLANTE: Oh, it's beautiful. It's pure gold isn't it, Targhetta? Where did you get it?

TARGHETTA: I got it a little while ago from a priest to give away on just such an occasion.

VIOLANTE: Oh, it's cute! Why don't you let me hold it in my hand a while? [*Aside*] If he gives it to me, that's the last he sees of it.

TARGHETTA: Women are never satisfied with just looking at something they like; they always want to hold it in their hands. Here it is.

VIOLANTE: Oh, look how pretty it is! Look how many bits and pieces there are inside. It looks exactly the same as the one I used to have. [*Aside*] You can cry your eyes out, now.

TARGHETTA: What is this about crying?

VIOLANTE: It looks exactly like the one that I lost and that made me cry so much. It has the same holes as mine, it's inlayed like mine,

the same size as mine—my goodness, it *is* mine.
TARGHETTA: Come off it.
VIOLANTE: No kidding, I've recognized it from the star inside the lid. Oh my trinket! You're welcome back; I thought you were lost forever.
TARGHETTA: Are you having me on? This one really takes the cake. Rest assured that I haven't stolen it for you. Tell me, where did you get yours from?
VIOLANTE: It was left to me by a generous Frenchman who stayed a while in my house and I kept it out of love for him.
TARGHETTA: A likely story! In that case you'd still have it.
VIOLANTE: No, I swear to God. I lent it to a monk so he could pluck the eyebrows of some girl of his; the other day, coming back from the monastery, it fell out of my bag. I had the priests announce that I'd lost it at sermon-time in all the churches; if you'd been at St. Francis' on Sunday, you'd have heard the preacher mention it.
TARGHETTA: Well, this one was lying in a monk's cell at the abbey and I grabbed it only an hour ago.
VIOLANTE: [*Aside*] I've got you now. —Well, this monk must be the sexton. It must have been returned to him yesterday, as the public notice stated that whoever found it, had to return it to him.
TARGHETTA: Give it here for a moment. Then you can go and ask the sexton.
VIOLANTE: Now that I think of it, I want to show it to my niece, Bita, who helps me with the washing. She kept it in her jewel box for a while so she's bound to recognise it if it's mine. Wait. [*Enters and closes the door.*]
TARGHETTA: Come back. Hey, why have you closed the door?
VIOLANTE: Because my doves are in here, and I don't want them to fly away and go missing like my vanity-case.
TARGHETTA: The pox on you, woman. You want to rob me of the vanity-case, you crafty old rascal.
VIOLANTE: The vanity-case is mine and you are the crafty one.[90] What next?
TARGHETTA: Give it back; open the door or I'll tear it down. [*Knock, knock.*]
VIOLANTE: Who's there? Who's knocking. What do you want, sir?
TARGHETTA: Do you think you're still young enough to play these tricks? I'm telling you, you are too old and this game doesn't

suit you. Do you think I'm going to let myself be fooled by you? Give me back my case.

VIOLANTE: [*Upstairs, at the window*] It's mine, mine, mine.[91] I can swear to it, I've got it in my hand. If you go and complain in court.[92] I'll tell them about that monk that you robbed.

TARGHETTA: [*Aside*] She's gone. I've only got what I deserved for playing around with a bawd I don't even like. Just look, now! She's not only tricked me but she's got away with it. Now I'd better change my tune, otherwise I'll be the loser. [*Knock, knock.*] —Hey, Violante, open up! Please! What does Bita say?

VIOLANTE: [*Opens up*] Here I am. Bita's sure that it's my case and that I'd be a fool to let it slip out of my hand.

TARGHETTA: Come on, let's find that nurse and give it to her.

VIOLANTE: I've found the nurse and I've resolved the ownership of the case: I'll be the nurse and you'll be the baby.[93]

TARGHETTA: Violante, don't make me angry; give me back my thing and then we'll see.

VIOLANTE: Do you really want it?

TARGHETTA: Certainly. Give it here.

VIOLANTE: Come closer if you want it.

TARGHETTA: Here I am. Give it to me.

VIOLANTE: Come closer. Here, take this, here's your thing, here's your washing. Ha, ha, ha.

(Violante strikes him in the face with a wet rag from the washing; with the other hand she throws ash on him and then she locks herself up in the house.)

TARGHETTA: You treacherous sow! [*Aside*] Look at the mess she's made: I'm all wet and covered with ash. Now I'll have to wait for the washing to dry. As soon as I try to be a lady-killer, I come off second best; she's treated me like a child and has taken me, in a cradle, to the nurse. And I certainly needed one! This is what happens to ill-gotten gains: they change hands again at once. But here's Carletto. I'd better hide this from him, otherwise he'll tell this joke to all my mates. Then they'll spread the word that I'm a solemn fool and I'll never be able to live it down. I'll take care of it. I don't want Violante to have to confess that she's obtained something from me or to go to that priest for penance.

SCENE IV

CARLETTO, TARGHETTA

CARLETTO: Targhetta, do you happen to know where my master is? I've waited more than an hour where he asked me to wait and he's not shown up; he must have been held up somewhere.
TARGHETTA: I've not seen him.
CARLETTO: Oh, you're covered in ash! What have you been up to?
TARGHETTA: I haven't done a thing. It's what others have done to me. I couldn't do anything about it. Do you know who lives there?
CARLETTO: People who carry swords but I know no more. Why?
TARGHETTA: Well now I'm done for. Just now, on my way here, somebody from that window threw ash on me. I'm sure it was all the ash from the washing. I was thinking of taking these people to court for the damages to my clothes, but if there are soldiers living here I'd better forget about the whole thing. By sending the bill here I risk being even worse off.[94] You can put this one down to experience.
CARLETTO: Too true. But tell me, do you think my master was at your place?
TARGHETTA: That isn't where I've come from, but I'd say not. Why do you think he'd hang around a mad bride?
CARLETTO: You're right. The poor young man is all upset. Even I feel so sad that I'm not myself any longer.
TARGHETTA: I believe you, I understand you. I'm not so chirpy myself, don't forget. This business is affecting both of us.
CARLETTO: Yes, good servants always share in their masters' misfortunes. But my master's in a worse fix than yours. Mine'll have to live with this mad woman for the rest of his life. Yours is getting rid of her.
TARGHETTA: Ha, ha, so that's how your mind is working! We weren't thinking of the same thing. My troubles aren't that kind at all. My problem is worse than yours. You're worrying about somebody else; I've got troubles of my own.
CARLETTO: Don't you believe me when I say that I suffer when my master suffers? What do I have more at heart than my master's interest?
TARGHETTA: What I have more at heart is my stomach which will be left full of wind. The luncheons, the banquets, the little luxu-

ries you can expect at a wedding, all those have gone overboard because of this disaster. You might have shown a bit of fellow-feeling on that score.

CARLETTO: Are you so insensitive as to think only of your belly at a time when our masters are in trouble?

TARGHETTA: What about you? Can you be such a fool as to worry about things that don't affect you?[95] You really have some odd ideas sometimes! Like the one you have about love: you think a person should have only one love affair. I think it would do everybody good to have several.

CARLETTO: That's true, I see it in my way and you see it in yours. And how does your way benefit everybody?

TARGHETTA: Plenty, because people die in many different ways but they're all born in the same way. So we must do our best to make sure that more people come into the world than go out ot it.

CARLETTO: What a stupid attitude!

TARGHETTA: You must be stupid if you worry more about others than about yourself. Don't you know that, since we are compelled to serve someone, we should serve with our body rather than our will?

CARLETTO: The true art of serving, Targhetta, is with the soul and not the body: otherwise gentlemen might as well have horses and mules for servants.

TARGHETTA: Aren't we treated like horses and mules? And if one of us were to kick his master, what do you think would happen?

CARLETTO: Then we'd really be animals. There's no greater bestiality in a servant than lack of patience and loyalty.

TARGHETTA: What is this loyalty? It's a word our masters are always using to make us serve them better. What loyalty should we have towards those who ill-treat us, who order us about as they like, who get angry with us without any reason, who make us suffer for our wages and who would sacrifice a hundred of our lives for a hunting-dog or a falcon?

CARLETTO: You also find masters who are loving and fair; I, for one, can say that I'm serving such a master.

TARGHETTA: Let me tell you this much: to serve somebody else is a profession a man takes up when there's nothing else going.

CARLETTO: On the contrary, you see lots of people who could have followed another profession, and could have lived at home like gentlemen, entering the service of one master or other and being

as happy as Larry.
TARGHETTA: You've said it: "They enter the service." You think only of those who enter; what happens when they leave it? They share the same fate as those who seek death in battle; they all end up the same way: dead. Can't you see that, without thinking of what they're doing, the moment they hear the drum rolling they jump in the air with delight. But when they come back, if any of them do, they're all crest-fallen, in tatters, penniless and half-crippled. That's exactly what happens to courtiers: after having spent their best years and used up all the money they can get from their families, they come back disillusioned, ashamed, in a pitiful condition, without a penny to their name and without having gained anything but an ulcer or some other illness.
CARLETTO: You also see a few who have grown rich and have done well for themselves.
TARGHETTA: These are the exceptions, like white crows. They distinguish themselves either because of their masters' caprices or because their bosses decided to act generously towards one, so as to lure others into their service and then trick them. Men are such fools that they prefer to think of one who has made it rather than a hundred who died in poverty.
CARLETTO: But if servants are paid and rewarded the moment they enter the service, they soon leave and plan to retire. That's why the masters delay paying them: so that they don't lose them.
TARGHETTA: But what a long delay it is! It's not until you're old or crippled and you can't pull the cart that you get some free time.[96] One thing which isn't done properly cancels out all the thousands which you have done perfectly. A pox on those who prefer to be slaves to others rather than being their own masters! If all servants joined forces, they would have to treat us well. How else could they manage?
CARLETTO: And if all masters agreed not to employ servants, how would we survive? How could a man without an income make ends meet?
TARGHETTA: And if they didn't have servants, how would they manage?
CARLETTO: Come now, you shouldn't enter someone's service if you aren't prepared to do it well. They're the masters and we're the servants. Nothing worse could happen than for us to think ourselves equal to them. I tell you, we should respect them, love

them and look after their possessions as if they were ours.
TARGHETTA: If they were willing for their things to be ours or at least to be shared, then we'd agree. But the thing is that they want everything for themselves, and since they want all the goodies for themselves we should also leave them all the bad things, like troubles and worries. When we have them, they don't pity us; they even add insult to injury.
CARLETTO: We'll never agree about this. Whenever my master suffers I suffer too.
TARGHETTA: And when mine suffers I'm happy, because then I can run the cellar the way I like. Since he's so absorbed in other matters, he won't notice how much wine I'm pilfering.
CARLETTO: I'd like my master to be always happy. Whenever I see him cheerful I feel happy myself. I must go now because I've got to go and see him.
TARGHETTA: I must go too. Before I go back home I want to go to that corner shop. And listen, wise man, don't take this world on your shoulders; it'll weigh on you too much, I'm telling you. Listen, Carletto, be more happy-go-lucky. Stop worrying. Otherwise you won't be worth a cent[97] and you'll suffer for it too.
CARLETTO: Well, each must live as he sees best. So long. [*Aside*] I'd better go and wait for my master at home. He's bound to come back for lunch; perhaps he's already back. It's late. [*Exit*]

SCENE V

MESSER FEDERIGO, TARGHETTA

MESSER FEDERIGO: [*Aside*] I've heard a strange thing: the more I mull it over the more I'm convinced that Madam Lepida is going through this performance because of me. She wants to get rid of this groom because she loves somebody else. This somebody else can't be anyone but me: I haven't seen any other suitor hanging around. I guessed right when I saw the nurse shut herself in the room with that pilgrim. They must have been talking about Lepida. But I couldn't get in quickly enough to that dark room with the cracks in the walls to be able to overhear everything right from the start. So what? The heart of the matter is this: I don't know what the nurse wanted from the pilgrim since when they came to the point, they withdrew, I don't know why, to another little room and I could hear no more. Anyhow, she must surely have me on her mind. There are no rivals. I've always had high hopes because of my contact through Targhetta. Gifts, letters, loving messages—all these count. She must surely be doing this for me, and all the more so since, according to the nurse, she keeps the name of this beloved hidden in her heart and has never agreed to reveal it to her.

TARGHETTA: [*Aside*] Those who carry appetising dishes should have the decency to cover them, so as not to make others die of envy. But some cruel people do the opposite—like those women who are too aware of their good figures and go out of their way to display them in order to slay those who are looking.

MESSER FEDERIGO: [*Aside*] But if this is how she feels, why doesn't she reveal the name, if not to the nurse at least to Targhetta, who knows all about our love?

TARGHETTA: [*Aside*] Some rascal came by me not long ago with a pair of pheasants, all nicely plucked, fattened and big. I noticed them and started to eye them off. The rogue saw this and, to torture me even more, he walked slowly; at last, to end my suffering, I plucked up courage and turned the corner. I thought I was admirably patient, given the circumstances.

MESSER FEDERIGO: [*Aside*] She must have had some good reason. Anyway, whether I'm the lucky one or not, I mustn't let this opportunity escape me. I must talk to her alone while things are still in suspense. Even if I were caught out, what harm could come of it?

TARGHETTA: [*Aside*] Oh, if only one could taste with one's eyes as much as with one's mouth, I'd have a ball, dirt cheap!

MESSER FEDERIGO: [*Aside*] I should act by the end of the day. But without Targhetta to give me an opportunity of getting near her, I can't do a thing. And I don't want to tell him what I've heard, since Lepida hasn't seen fit to trust anyone, why should I? But here he comes. This must be a good omen. —What are you up to, Targhetta?

TARGHETTA: My good lord, whatever your Lordship wishes. I'm always happy when I see you and I love no other country more than Germany. You're royal, generous, liberal; I like your way of drinking, and of sitting for five or six hours over a meal! I'm at your service.

MESSER FEDERIGO: And I like you because I see that you're taking to

our customs. Now tell me, on your life: do you think that Madam Lepida loves me at all?
TARGHETTA: You upset me when you ask me such things. I'd have thought you already had enough proof of it.
MESSER FEDERIGO: I saw her not long ago in church and she turned the other way the moment she saw me.
TARGHETTA: No wonder! She's lost her wits!
MESSER FEDERIGO: She always makes a point of ignoring me whenever she sees me from her window or in the streets.
TARGHETTA: Maybe in Germany women are all made the same way, but in Tuscany there's a great difference between them. There are some who sit at the window but only look and sneer; if they meet you in the streets they turn their face away ten times, taking pleasure in doing this at every corner they meet you. There are others who ignore you if they see you alone; but if you're at a banquet or a party, they introduce you to people, they invite you to dance just to appear popular and in demand; they find excuses to talk to you and they carry on with a hundred stupidities which mean nothing. There are others still who are sensisble enough to avoid all public display. They pretend not to see those they love either when they're at the window or in the streets or at parties or in church; but they work secretly at what they want with messages, letters and tête-à-têtes. Lepida belongs to this last group: she hates shows of affection which, in fact, are women's downfall.
MESSER FEDERIGO: I don't think she belongs to either group. She's always avoided any kind of demonstration of affection and she hasn't given me any sign of favour.
TARGHETTA: I'll tell you, my lord, out of the experience I've had of these things after having served many women, one must realize that there are several types of women who want to please their lovers. Some provide your opportunity themselves; others expect you to look for it. Others try to please you in their own way, and you won't achieve anything by being importunate or using force; others, on the contrary, behave like the besieged inhabitants of a castle! They think that, before they can surrender with honour, they must stand an assault or two. There are others still who are so irresolute, shy and devoid of willpower that they don't dare do anything, even if they'd like to; the only way with them is to force them. You can be sure that my little mistress belongs to this

last type.

MESSER FEDERIGO: To be honest, I had already reached this conclusion myself and I wanted to see you to talk to you about it; I've decided to try something out and I want you to get me into her place.

TARGHETTA: This isn't the right moment, now that she's lost her wits. Let's wait four days until she's cured.

MESSER FEDERIGO: Targhetta, if you've ever received favours from me, if you hope to gain any more—and you will—you've got to find a way to introduce me into her chamber. You've kept me waiting too long.

TARGHETTA: [*Aside*] I've got my back to the wall now. Shall I do it or not? I shall. Anyhow she's mad.

MESSER FEDERIGO: What are you saying?

TARGHETTA: I'm saying that I don't know what you want to do now that she's mad.

MESSER FEDERIGO: I want to take a pledge of her love now so that she'll be mine when she's come to her senses.

TARGHETTA: I'll do what you want. But this is like one of those fancies, some other men have had, of wanting to have sex with a woman who's already unconscious or dead.

MESSER FEDERIGO: I'm determined to do it. Think up a plan.

TARGHETTA: I can't think of a better way than to get you there by the spiral staircase after you've got in through that small door, on the ground floor, which opens onto the back yard. That's the door which is always locked: I think you know which one.

MESSER FEDERIGO: Yes, I understand; it's a good way. I want to do it today if possible. Make sure you open that little door. I'll enter the house pretending to go and see the master and, if I happen not to be seen by anyone, I'll soon reach the spiral staircase.

TARGHETTA: That's it. After you've got into the yard and climbed the staircase, go straight in. That's her bedroom.

MESSER FEDERIGO: I get it. Go home now and don't lose a minute. I want to go and look after some business and when I find the right moment I'll come.

TARGHETTA: [*Aside*] Things haven't turned out so badly. I couldn't hold this gentleman back any longer anyway. Lepida's crazy. If he doesn't find things as I've described them, he'll think it's because she's lost her wits and he won't think I've tricked him. And if, by chance, since she's beyond herself, he gets what he wants, I'm bound to get a good tip. Now I'd better go home and see what I can do for the gentleman. [*Enters Lepida's house*]

MESSER FEDERIGO: [*Aside*] Things are going well. If I can find her alone in that room I'll certainly find out whether I'm the one for whom she's putting on this performance. If I were to be found there, I wouldn't suffer the same fate as those caught by surprise in similar circumstances: where they would be ruined, I shall gain. The husband will be even less anxious to have her if she's caught with a man in her room. And the father, seeing that she's out of her senses and repudiated by her other man, will only be too happy to give her to me. Well, while I'm waiting to get myself ino Mistress Lepida's house, I'd better go to the baths. I'll call my servant.

SCENE VI

MESSER FEDERIGO, a German; CAVICCHIA, his servant

MESSER FEDERIGO: [*In the street*] Cavicchia, come down here!

CAVICCHIA: [*Inside*] Yes sir, straight away.

MESSER FEDERIGO: [*Aside*] If I don't take a bath on my usual day, I don't feel comfortable.

CAVICCHIA: [*Now downstairs*] What are your Lordship's wishes?

MESSER FEDERIGO: I want to go to the baths; find me a white shirt and a pair of shoes.

CAVICCHIA: I'll also find two towels, four pieces of cloth, and the sheet for when you come out of the bath since the baths attendant doesn't have any soft linen. And I also want to take your perfumed soap. You remember, last time he used an awful soap which smelled of resin.

MESSER FEDERIGO: Whatever you think. But don't forget to bring those new stockings I wore the other morning, and make sure you get there before I finish bathing.

CAVICCHIA: I'll do that. That baths attendant should take a bit more trouble and line up a fine lady to dry your Lordship and caress you while you rest.

MESSER FEDERIGO: Go away, you ass! Do you think a lady would ever come and do these things to her lover at the public baths? You ignorant fellows don't know what true ladies are like.

CAVICCHIA: Forgive me, but I know them better than you. It's pseudo-nobles like you who don't know which type of women men should choose to love.

MESSER FEDERIGO: Which type should that be, Mr. Know-all?

CAVICCHIA: As long as you stay away from married women, widows and respectable young girls, you can't go wrong.

MESSER FEDERIGO: Who does that leave?

CAVICCHIA: Courtesans, serving-maids and loose women.

MESSER FEDERIGO: Courtesans? What's the good of going where the populace goes? One must have a woman to oneself.

CAVICCHIA: When you're in the middle of your business, you're the only one who counts. My lord, to want something that's hard to get is a way of never getting what you want. You run many risks when you deal with a noble woman, so what's the good of doing it? Can't you see how many guards, how many suspicions you must overcome to enjoy the company of a noblewoman once in a blue moon?

MESSER FEDERIGO: One of those triumphs is worth a thousand of your kind.

CAVICCHIA: And even then you can't really enjoy what you've won. A jolt, a sneeze, the barking of a dog, a murmur can ruin your life and your honour while with a courtesan there is nothing but sweetness. You can go and visit her whenever you wish, in the daytime or at night by the light of a torch, exactly when you feel like it. And if you have had your fill or she annoys you, you can either leave or give her a kick, while these noblewomen are so haughty and full of themselves that they expect to be continuously adored. Besides, courtesans are more pleasing, more experienced in cajoling and caressing; and when they feel like it, they even come and look for you. With them you don't run the risk of having to scuttle under a bed or into a coffer at the risk of crippling yourself whenever something goes wrong.

MESSER FEDERIGO: You don't know anything about anything. A smile, a glance from a noblewoman makes up for all the discomfort and loss which could follow.

CAVICCHIA: I'm telling you that an oily flat loaf prepared by a maid with a bit of garlic or the dishwater that rubs off on you when she comes near is worth more than all the ceremonies and perfumes of one of your stuffy lovers.

MESSER FEDERIGO: Don't say any more; you've given me a headache.

CAVICCHIA: Do you expect to get rid of it by going to talk to that boring tutor?

MESSER FEDERIGO: I must go and see him before it's dark; I always learn something new from him.
CAVICCHIA: Ah yes? Just like the bit of academic pedantry I quoted, which made me look like a simpleton among my mates at the inn the other day.
MESSER FEDERIGO: How did that happen?
CAVICCHIA: I'll tell you: since the conversation fell on the stars and how many of them there could be, I said that astrologers kept count of no more than a thousand stars. (I heard the tutor say that to you one day). Everybody burst out laughing and said: "What? The ones seen in Pisa are ten times that number without counting those you see in Rome, Venice, Milan and many other places...."
MESSER FEDERIGO: He knows what he's talking about and he doesn't talk through his hat. Now keep quiet and don't talk of matters which you don't understand. Go and fetch what I need and come quickly to the baths. [*Exit*]
CAVICCHIA: I will. [*Exit*]

SCENE VII

GIGLIETTA, VIOLANTE

GIGLIETTA: My word, Violante, this pilgrim is a kind soul. I simply adore her and I can't wait for her to see Lepida.
VIOLANTE: Isn't she the way I said? What do you think of the other matter now that you've examined her? Did she appear to be the way I described her to you?
GIGLIETTA: Not really. Listen to me, she's doing this pilgrimage out of love, remember, and she's got something on her mind. When we were talking of a particular detail regarding a love matter I heard a sigh which was really genuine. So don't make any plans for her, because she has noble ideas in her head.
VIOLANTE: Amidst noble thoughts there are often some lower-class ones. I see plenty of young men who in the daylight court a noblewoman and at night have a good time with some little tart. Some women do exactly the same thing.
GIGLIETTA: Believe me, she isn't one of them; on the contrary, she's all devoted to spiritual matters and she's obsessed by a love that won't go away.

VIOLANTE: To the devil with her love! Let's talk of ours: it's a long time since we've discussed it. Tell me the truth, Giglietta, you're enjoying yourself with that handsome tutor in your household, aren't you? Well, good luck to you. Maids have a right to tutors and manservants.
GIGLIETTA: They should, but sometimes our mistresses take away our rights. Not in my case, though!
VIOLANTE: I can tell you, if it wasn't for my friendship for you, I'd have tried to have it off with him.
GIGLIETTA: He's got other things on his mind.
VIOLANTE: What should I do?
GIGLIETTA: I'm telling you I haven't anything going with him. You help yourself. I've never had much time for academic types.
VIOLANTE: You've never tried one; if you had, you wouldn't talk that way. There's no sweeter affair than one with a student.
GIGLIETTA: I've never wanted to try it. I've always believed the saying: "Studies and pleasures don't mix."[98] Besides, these students look pale, tired, melancholic and quite unsuited to women.
VIOLANTE: Let me tell you, they appear like that on the outside, but if you know how to handle them, you can't do better. You know I've tried all types; I swear to you I never had it better than that whole year I spent with a student. I still cry when I think of him: he was gallant! A trickster, a scoundrel, a jail-bird! He never made love to me twice in the same way: a man full of imagination, of new ways. Only those who read books find out about these things, and if I know anything, I owe it to him.
GIGLIETTA: As you like. I once heard a doctor's wife say that if she had twenty daughters, she would have strangled them rather than marry them to doctors because she didn't want them to suffer as she had.
VIOLANTE: She must have run into a fool of a doctor, suffering from consumption and withered with old age; not all are like that. How many women, do you think, are satisfied with their choice? To conclude, the way the students behave is exceptional. They're as faithful as a dog and secretive as a fish. If some little problem occurs, as sometimes happens, they find a thousand ways to save and conceal everything.
GIGLIETTA: I don't know about that; but I do know that they're always shut away indoors, bent over books. I myself . . .
VIOLANTE: But that's a point in their favour, since, when you don't see

your lad, you can be certain he isn't out having a good time and you always have him locked up in there at your disposal. What can you do with these good-for-nothing idlers who strut around the place all day displaying their chests like cock pigeons and their heads like peacocks? And after they've said to you—I'm at your service; I'm at your command—they don't know what to do with themselves.
GIGLIETTA: If you like students so much you must have what you want right in your house. That German fellow, Master Federigo, doesn't look too bad.
VIOLANTE: These Germans, for your information, are not much fun.
GIGLIETTA: However they're soft, white like dough and ready for action.
VIOLANTE: True, but with women they're cold and rigid, and wouldn't feel anything even if you tickled them.
GIGLIETTA: Violante, I'd stay here all day to listen to you and I'd forget to go home where I've a thousand things to do. I'll see you again when I can, since I enjoy talking about these things.
VIOLANTE: Please do, so that we can at least put into words what we can't actually do. Farewell. [*Exit*]
GIGLIETTA: [*Aside*] My goodness: she must be telling the truth when she talks about students since I see that Lepida is madly in love with Messer Terenzio. Now let me go and console them a bit with the news that this pilgrim will willingly help us as we want. [*Exit*]

SCENE VIII

CASSANDRO, VIOLANTE, RICCIARDO, PILGRIM

CASSANDRO: [*Aside*] One mustn't hurry when one goes to lawyers or solicitors. Since I didn't find Lucrezio at home a while ago, I went to Messer Cino's house to get some information about this new case. I stayed there a while but I couldn't talk to him. There were twenty-five people around him, one to make a protest against a bill, another to take out a libel action, others to produce documents, to take out a summons, and so on. These lawyers are a devilish torment, by God! Small wonder they cost people their wealth and even their lives, not to mention their wits and their souls.

VIOLANTE: [*Aside*] This job of looking after a boarding house is killing me! You're forever cleaning here, drying there. Now you shake this, now you put away that. Look at the state that curtain is in!
CASSANDRO: [*Aside*] Well now, since I haven't achieved anything with the lawyers, I'd better talk to this pilgrim.
VIOLANTE: [*Aside*] Look at this hole! That ass Cavicchia must have done this. I think the rascal put his spurs on and then went to bed.
CASSANDRO: [*Aside*] Violante is at the window. —Violante, could I have a word with the pilgrim staying at your house?
VIOLANTE: Just a moment. Giglietta has just left and a while before your son-in-law came. [*Exit*]
CASSANDRO: [*Aside*] Lucrezio has been here? But that's awful! Giglietta must have seen him and has run to inform the pilgrim. It was a good idea to warn her. I can say this in all honesty: the two people I've got in my house, the tutor and the nurse, are without equals. Messer Terenzio has an attachment, a love for this house as if it belonged to his own family; Giglietta has always taught my Lepida good manners and habits as if she were her own daughter. I know she hasn't filled her head with stupidities and talk: she's always in her room looking after Lepida's affairs for her.
RICCIARDO: Sir, my lady the pilgrim is coming down. Are you perchance the father of that bride who lives nearby?
CASSANDRO: Yes sir. Are you perhaps a relative of this pilgrim?
RICCIARDO: Not a blood relative, but more than a relative in my love for her, since I grew up in her household.
PILGRIM: [*Now downstairs*] What does this gentleman want from me?
RICCIARDO: You'll hear it from him. He's the father of that young girl you've already heard about.
PILGRIM: I see. Sir, I can guess what you want from me. I don't profess to be a doctor but I've a few secret remedies, as I've said to your son-in-law; since we're bound to help each other, I willingly offer my services, but don't expect more of me than what I'm worth.
CASSANDRO: I know you're worth a lot and I haven't any other hope but you to avoid losing a son-in-law and a daughter.
PILGRIM: You've certainly given her a very attractive husband. Perhaps there will be someone who, taking advantage of her illness, will try to get him away, just as you might have snatched him from someone who had her eyes on him.
CASSANDRO: There was indeed some competition. But how can we

set about curing her?
PILGRIM: I can't start anything until I see the young girl herself.
CASSANDRO: I thought as much myself and I wanted to tell you that it'd be advisable, if it's convenient, for you to come and see her now.
PILGRIM: I'm available whenever it suits you: let's go now. Come with us, Ricciardo.
RICCIARDO: Yes, madam. Do you want me to fetch the bottles of oil?
PILGRIM: It doesn't matter, for the time being. It will suffice if I can see her. I see that you're downcast, my good old man, and perhaps you've reason to be. But cheer up.
CASSANDRO: You're making me feel better already.
RICCIARDO: Is this your house?
CASSANDRO: Yes sir.
RICCIARDO: It seems a very good house. It's satisfying to live well.
CASSANDRO: Among the ancient houses of our city I can say that I've a very comfortable one. But just as one lives well in a hut if one's mind is free from worries, so someone who's afflicted, as I am, lives badly even in the most comfortable of palaces.
RICCIARDO: We know from experience that good fortune doesn't last forever, so we must hope that ill fortune doesn't stay around forever either.
CASSANDRO: I'll lead the way.
RICCIARDO: We'll follow you. [*Exeunt*]

SCENE IX

CAVICCHIA, VIOLANTE

CAVICCHIA: [*In the street*] Either I leave him or he leaves your house.
VIOLANTE: [*Inside*] Either he throws you out or I throw him out of my house. Is this the way to behave, ruining my bed-curtains? Let him come back and, as soon as he's back, I'll tell him about all your rotten tricks.
CAVICCHIA: Let him come back! As soon as he's back, I want to talk to him about your little tricks.
VIOLANTE: And whatever can you say about me?
CAVICCHIA: What can be said of a slut like you. What can you say about me?

VIOLANTE: What can be said of the most wicked servant ever to be found. This German must be the poorest man in the world because if he had what it takes to employ a worthy servant, he'd never have you.
CAVICCHIA: It's the other way round. He must be the richest because, if he hadn't money to throw away, he wouldn't waste ten scudi per month on such a vile boarding house. If he didn't eat with his ears and drink with his nose, he'd never last it out.[99] You always dish out warmed up soups, goat meat instead of mutton, beef instead of veal; game and birds have been banned. All the glassware, glasses and carafes and similar things seem dressed for battle since they're wearing armour.[100] Tablecloths and table napkins are changed every new moon, once a month.
VIOLANTE: People who live in glass houses shouldn't throw the first stone![101] I've never seen a dirtier person than you; only a few days ago you put your dirty spurs on your master's white shirts.
CAVICCHIA: And what about you? You never wash the kitchenware: you just let the dog lick it clean.
VIOLANTE: There's no need for a dog while we've got you. You always go around cleaning up all the kitchen pots with your hands and snout and then, when you're all dirty and greasy, help the master to get dressed.
CAVICCHIA: And how does this vixen treat us in other matters? There is never good wine on the table. It either tastes of vinegar or it's turned bad or it's gone off.
VIOLANTE: Go and hang yourself! Didn't your master say the other morning that the wine was very good?
CAVICCHIA: Good? Yes. It had no sins since it had just been christened with water.[102] What a holy person! She's performing miracles now: water turns into wine, and even the watered down wine is in pretty short supply.
VIOLANTE: What do you expect? Do you want to have a flask always hanging from your bedstead, you drunkard?
CAVICCHIA: And what do you think? That I want to serve a German without doing him honour?
VIOLANTE: Never again will I offer full board to anyone. I'll just offer lodgings like I do for the others. I agreed to make an exception for this fellow because of his insistence, but I've struck a bad bargain.
CAVICCHIA: Sure, sure, you prefer to offer lodgings, don't you? When

you land some simpleton, who hasn't a servant to look after him, you surely clean him out, don't you? If he does his own shopping, you steal half of the stuff; if he asks you to buy him something, you steal half of the money.

VIOLANTE: Do you think everybody behaves the way you do to your master? You rotten slanderer. I'll gouge out one of your eyes, one day.

CAVICCHIA: Really! What on earth would you do if you were a ball of fire?

VIOLANTE: I'd throw myself on you and burn you up.

CAVICCHIA: And I'd piss on you and put you out.

VIOLANTE: I know very well why you're always at your worst.

CAVICCHIA: Why?

VIOLANTE: Because I've never done what you wanted.

CAVICCHIA: And do you know why you hate me?

VIOLANTE: Why?

CAVICCHIA: Because I've never given a stuff for you.

VIOLANTE: Your withered little affair[103] doesn't interest me in the least.

CAVICCHIA: And your smelly little violet[104] isn't my kind of flower either.

VIOLANTE: You rogue, come inside, come in and I'll shave your beard off.

CAVICCHIA: Come outside, come out and I'll cut your clothes at the waist.[105]

VIOLANTE: Stop bragging! Don't forget I'm capable of cutting you up.

CAVICCHIA: Wait, wait and you'll soon see I'm man enough to cut your nose off. You talk like this because you can see that I'm carrying things. Let me take them to the baths where my master is and then I'll show you I've more brains than you.

VIOLANTE: You scoundrel! You dare to come back! Just dare! [*Exeunt*]

SCENE X

CASSANDRO, PILGRIM, RICCIARDO

CASSANDRO: Now that the poor sick girl can't hear us and we can talk freely, what can you tell me? What do you think?

PILGRIM: I'll be frank with you. It's a serious and complicated sickness; it's madness of the worst kind. It's true that God's grace is infinite and that it performs miracles in such cases, but if she doesn't benefit from a cure I've thought of administering to her, then I've little hope of her recovering.

RICCIARDO: [*Aside*] She speaks with the voice of one who's practised medicine for a thousand years!

CASSANDRO: My Lord, what a tragedy this is! And what are you thinking of doing?

PILGRIM: I want her to take a bath in some miraculous herbs: they will calm her down and make her recover her wits.

RICCIARDO: Isn't this the way you cured that other woman in Spain?

PILGRIM: That's right.

RICCIARDO: And she was raving mad! [*Aside*] Since we have to carry off this pretence, I want to help too.

PILGRIM: We'll have to spend some money—though I don't think you're worried about that.

CASSANDRO: Not at all. I'm prepared to spend any amount provided she's cured.

PILGRIM: We'll try this bath, then, and if it doesn't work I'd advise you to break off the marriage and keep on telling her that she no longer has a husband; I know that the idea of getting married has worried her so much that she's lost her wits.

CASSANDRO: I'd like to wait as long as I can before breaking off the marriage since I won't have the face to try to find her another husband in Pisa. And if the marriage has to be broken off, I'd rather the groom did it than me. But I think you're right about making her think the wedding is off. I'll go along with that.

PILGRIM: I don't think there's anything else for the time being. You get a basin large enough for her to immerse her entire body in, and in the meantime I'll go to the druggist to look for some precious perfumes which we must boil with the herbs. Furthermore, I'll order someone to fetch a certain herb, known to only a few; I know they don't keep it in the shops but I saw plenty of it on the banks of the Arno on our way to Pisa.

CASSANDRO: I'm sorry you've to go to so much trouble because of me; I'll be all the more indebted to you.

PILGRIM: I do it all quite willingly. Don't worry about it. You can go now if you have some business to attend to. Don't forget the basin and leave the rest to me.

CASSANDRO: When do you think of administering this bath?
PILGRIM: I'll prepare things today, then tomorow, with God's help, we'll bath her.
CASSANDRO: Yes, early in the morning. I'll go and see my son-in-law now. [*Exit*]
PILGRIM: Goodbye, then.
RICCIARDO: My word, you really sound like an experienced doctor. Who taught you all this?
PILGRIM: The most perfect masters one can find: necessity and love.
RICCIARDO: If this madness is feigned, as you've said, why go through all this?
PILGRIM: We must show that we're trying out some remedy and convince them afterwards that it hasn't worked. Then Lucrezio will have a proper reason to leave her and this young girl may get what she wants. If you'd seen her when I drew her alone into her room and she threw herself at my feet, you'd have cried.
RICCIARDO: How clever she is! When she was with us, she pretended to be a fool!
PILGRIM: I assure you that I'd have helped her even if I didn't have a vested interest because I admire her courage.
RICCIARDO: Her courage is certainly remarkable. I wonder which one of you two has given greater demonstration of love: you, by setting out on such a long pilgrimage, or she, by feigning to be mad.
PILGRIM: She's given great proof of her love, but I think mine is even greater. See how opposite are our aims in this situation. I do what I am doing to gain Lucrezio and she to get rid of him.
RICCIARDO: Certainly you are at opposite ends. Let's go this way because I think there's a herborist shop here.
PILGRIM: Let's go. [*Exeunt*]

SCENE XI

MESSER FEDERIGO alone

I don't know whether I've washed with water or with fire in those baths. I feel so oppressed by a constant burning pang of anxiety. What's going on? With my body I'm nearing my lady's house to carry out my resolution and with my mind I'm drawing away and going back. What suspicion, what shadow, what fear am I creating? If I thought that in that staircase I've to climb or in that room I've to enter there was a dragon spitting fire all around, or that there was an army of a thousand enemies, or that there was hell itself (if hell can exist in the same place where such a beautiful girl lives), I'd go bravely. Now that I'm proceeding with the hope of finding a woman alone, why am I fearful, trembling? Whatever it is, I must go. In the end it's better that I should die because of her disdain than out of my stupidity. I think I'll go this way so that I can enter unnoticed from the garden door and then I'll reach the spiral staircase straight away.

ACT IV

SCENE I

TARGHETTA, CASSANDRO

TARGHETTA: [*Aside*] I always knew that women learned to deceive before they learned to talk. I always thought that they could cry and faint whenever they wished, and that a wife could caress her husband as if she meant it even if she didn't love him. All this I knew; what I didn't know was that they could masquerade in such a big way. I certainly did not expect it of a young girl like Lepida who's still wet behind the ears. After I opened the small door leading to the winding staircase, as I agreed with the German, I heard people talking in that room. I squatted down so as not to be seen, and I soon realized that these good women had come there to talk in private. By pricking up my ears, I heard from them that this madness was a front put on to please Lucrezio, that they've known each other for a while, and that they're friends. I wonder if she acted hostile the first night he came to the house, as if she hadn't seen him before! Upon my word, women are absolute daughters of deception! I withdrew in a hurry: I was dying to give this good piece of news to my master so that I could gain something from it. The poor old man has been more dead than alive from the moment they began to make him suffer with this pantomime. But here he comes. I'd better make out like I've been running to find him.

CASSANDRO: [*Aside*] A man tires easily when he exerts his body and has worries, especially when he's old like me. I've been traipsing around since this morning.

TARGHETTA: Welcome, master. Chee . . . cheer up, goo . . . good news.[106]

CASSANDRO: What's up? You seem out of breath.
TARGHETTA: Let me gather my breath. I'm out of it, all right. Everything will be fine.
CASSANDRO: Come on, tell me. What's good about this news?
TARGHETTA: As long as you give me a tip—I know you'll think I deserve it.
CASSANDRO: I'll give you whatever you want. Don't keep me on tenterhooks.
TARGHETTA: I've found out what makes Lepida appear to be crazy.
CASSANDRO: Instead you should find someone who can cure her. What do you mean? Come on, tell!
TARGHETTA: She can be cured by the person who caused her madness. Now, I want you to listen carefully to this strange thing.
CASSANDRO: Please, don't keep me waiting any longer.
TARGHETTA: Lepida isn't mad at all, she's only pretending.
CASSANDRO: Pretending? Now it's you who are mad. Why should she be pretending?
TARGHETTA: To please her husband.
CASSANDRO: Whom, Lucrezio?[107]
TARGHETTA: Yes sir, Lucrezio.
CASSANDRO: Come off it; Lucrezio is so fed up that he's about to repudiate her.
TARGHETTA: Repudiate her, my foot. I tell you, he's the one behind all this.
CASSANDRO: How have they been able to plot all this together? They've hardly spoken to each other and they only met four days ago.
TARGHETTA: Four days! If you had said four months, you'd have guessed better.
CASSANDRO: Alas, what are you saying? Four months? God help me.
TARGHETTA: Soon you'll see what follows from this.
CASSANDRO: Hurry up once and for all. Tell me quickly how the matter stands.
TARGHETTA: Well, while I was going a while ago into the new room to fetch the key for the granary—because I wanted to sweep up that grain so that it wouldn't go bad—well, while I was looking for it behind the bed where it usually is, Lepida and the nurse came in. Since they didn't see me, they started whispering and, among other things, I heard Lepida say these words: You can say what you want, nurse; though this feigned madness is taking its toll on me, nevertheless, out of love for Lucrezio who desires it,

I'd do even more as long as by doing it I can hide my pregnancy.
CASSANDRO: Lepida is pregnant? Lepida is pregnant? This is the news you think worthy of a tip?
TARGHETTA: Yes sir. Shouldn't married women be pregnant?
CASSANDRO: Should a young girl behave like this without her father's knowledge?
TARGHETTA: Did you want her to call you?
CASSANDRO: Don't try to distract me.
TARGHETTA: I think I know how things went. They must have gone to bed together; they must have met at night time like cats and Lucrezio, like the fine young man he is, must have asked her to marry him.
CASSANDRO: This is the way things are. We have to accept it. Come on, let's let things follow their course then. Let them do as they please; they won't ever have my blessing again. Why did they have to resort to such tricks? Why did she pretend to be mad, and why did he make out that he didn't want her any longer? Why should they give me this worry?
TARGHETTA: Haven't you heard what Lepida was saying? They wanted to hide her pregnancy because they would have been ashamed if you had found out.
CASSANDRO: Wasn't there any other way to do this? If they couldn't think of anything else, why didn't he take her home straight away? I still can't find an explanation for all this that satisfies me.
TARGHETTA: If she's pregnant, you'll soon find a reason. Who knows? Perhaps Lucrezio has made her feign this madness and then has said that he didn't want her any more so as to increase the dowry by a thousand ducati. You must remember that he's a merchant and this is a trick that's typical of merchants.
CASSANDRO: You could be right. It can't be otherwise, I'm sure you're right. But I'd never have expected my daughter to hurt me like this, especially this year when the grain is going off. What has this world come to! Young girls forget their fathers at the drop of a hat, and give themselves totally to their husbands. Once, love for one's father and mother was of the utmost importance. Look at the way I've been duped! Today I've earned the money that was to be given to them. Not a word of this to anyone at home; it's better that no one knows about it. I want to be the first one to talk about it with Lucrezio. I shall go and look for him again until I find him.

TARGHETTA: Do as you think is best. What do you say now? Don't I deserve a tip since I made you save so much?
CASSANDRO: Yes, certainly. Remind me this Christmas and I won't forget my promise. Now that I remember, go to that druggist where you'll find the pilgrim. Tell her not to worry any longer about the bath or the medicines since Lepida doesn't need them any more. If she asks you why, tell her I'll explain later. Don't waste any time, otherwise I'll have to settle this debt with the druggist as well. [*Exit*]
TARGHETTA: I'm on my way. [*Aside*] This poor old man has half recovered, I tell you. They sure wanted to dupe him and take him for a ride!

SCENE II

RICCIARDO, PILGRIM, TARGHETTA

RICCIARDO: I know that you'll have astonished this druggist by the number of things you've asked for. But that little one who's a herbalist insists that that herb isn't to be found around here. So how come you've seen it?
PILGRIM: That's the least of their mistakes. First doctors grope in the dark and then, if by chance they hit on something sensible, everything is spoiled by ignorant druggists. One should strive never to fall into their hands!
TARGHETTA: [*Aside*] How lucky I was to have run into Palandra, who told me he saw this pilgrim in Cacciarella street: he saved me a bit of road. I'll go this way to meet her.
RICCIARDO: Well said. The few times I had to place myself in the hands of doctors, I did it more because it was expected of me than out of faith in them.
TARGHETTA: [*Aside*] They were extolling the virtues of this quack to the sky. She insisted that Lepida was mad and wanted to bath her—claimed that it would certainly have brought out the 'madness' which she had in her body. She never realized that Lepida was cannier than she was since she couldn't even detect her pregnancy. Here she comes.
PILGRIM: What can this man want who's coming towards us?
TARGHETTA: My lady, I'm sent by Cassandro, my master, to tell you that no bath is needed any longer and that you should forget about

it.

PILGRIM: Why? The ingredients have already been ordered.

TARGHETTA: Cancel the order since they are no longer needed. The bride is cured and she's so sane that she could sell her wisdom to others.

PILGRIM: I'd like it to be true; but how can she be well all of a sudden?

TARGHETTA: That's the way it is. I was the one who, without soaring too high, found the jar with her wits in it.[108]

RICCIARDO: You'd be a good specialist if you really could restore people's wits just like that. My friend, one can't know so quickly if somebody is cured or not.

PILGRIM: This is particularly true with cases of madness. She might appear for a while to be sane and to be herself again and then start carrying on again like a madwoman.

TARGHETTA: Doctors always dislike sanity. I'm telling you she's sane, perfectly sane. Tell me which druggist I have to contact to cancel your prescriptions.

PILGRIM: [Aside] They must have discovered something. —Tell me, please, exactly how things stand.

TARGHETTA: You'll learn everything from my master. I don't want to waste time here.

PILGRIM: You can't treat me like this. You have to tell me now; do me the favour.

TARGHETTA: [Aside] Now, now, she's truly disappointed to be taken off this case! I think I'll tell her so that she'll really lose her temper. What does it matter to the master? —In a few words, Lepida's madness was feigned.

PILGRIM: [Aside] It's as I expected: the game is up. —I thought that much, the moment I saw her, but I didn't think it was up to me to say anything.

TARGHETTA: Yes, yes, I see: so that the case wouldn't come to a quick end.

PILGRIM: Tell me, do you know why she was putting on this performance?

TARGHETTA: I do. It's really strange that you didn't know since you can work everything out. I'll explain it to you. Lucrezio made love to Lepida before marrying her and now she's already a few months pregnant.

PILGRIM: I see it all! Ricciardo. [She's about to faint]

RICCIARDO: [To the pilgrim] Don't show your emotions now. Listen

to the rest.
TARGHETTA: Now listen to me! I haven't finished yet! Now that he has decided to marry her, he makes her pretend to be mad for two reasons: to cover up her pregnancy and, with this trick, to ask for more dowry from his father-in-law.
PILGRIM: Do you know this for sure?
TARGHETTA: What do you mean, for sure? I've heard it from her very mouth when she was talking about it not long ago with the nurse, unaware that I was listening.
PILGRIM: It must be so, then. Now go to the druggist or wherever you want.
TARGHETTA: Which druggist ?
PILGRIM: The 'Fortuna'. Go!
TARGHETTA: [*Walking away. Aside*] That upset her enough! But what a fool I am! Now that I think of it, I haven't gone to see the German to tell him not to go after all. I hope I'm still in time.
PILGRIM: It seemed a thousand years before that servant went and I could cry and inveigh against such a cruel man. Ah, ungrateful Lucrezio! Wicked Lucrezio! Now I know your deceit. Now I see your lies clearly. Now I understand why you didn't return to Valencia. With what intentions did you start loving this new bride? To deceive her, just as you've done with me? What loyalty did you promise her, you horrible man? The same type which you pledged to me and then betrayed? Since God keeps you alive, why did you perjure yourself in such a way? May other women learn from me not to believe tears, sighs and lovers' oaths since they're all false and deceitful.
RICCIARDO: Please, my lady, let's go home; I don't want anyone to hear you say such things in the middle of the street! At home you can let yourself go as you wish.
PILGRIM: I want the whole town to hear me so that they'll know of the betrayal perpetrated by that ungrateful man. Here, Drusilla, is what you set out for: to see your woe with your own eyes and to be present when the man, who by rights is yours, leaves you to give himself to another woman. Alas, since forgetfulness hasn't put an end to my suffering, I hope that death will.
RICCIARDO: Let's go home, please; you can't even stand upright because of the pain. Can't you see?
PILGRIM: Ah, each word spoken by that man has been a blow to my heart.

RICCIARDO: Let's go inside; I hope you'll learn to hate this wicked man as much as you've loved him. Legitimate resentment can turn the most ardent love into hate. Lean on me since you can't stand on your own feet. [*Exeunt*]

SCENE III

LUCREZIO, CASSANDRO

LUCREZIO: [*Aside*] How is it possible to spend the whole day looking for Cassandro and not find him? I'll have to go and look for him at his home which I had decided not to enter again. The pilgrim's mission is very important to me and it could spoil everything to send her there without warning him.
CASSANDRO: [*Aside*] Where on earth has my son-in-law got to? I've decided to tell him exactly the way I feel. How thoughtless it is to inflict such worry on an old man! But here he is. —Where are you going, Lucrezio?
LUCREZIO: I was looking for you. I can't tell you how worried I am because of Lepida's illness.
CASSANDRO: I've noticed it. Thank God you are worried!
LUCREZIO: May God be my witness in what I intend to do.
CASSANDRO: What you've done so far is quite enough.
LUCREZIO: So far I haven't done a thing except with my intentions and my words.
CASSANDRO: You've done something more concrete than that.
LUCREZIO: Has that pilgrim perchance gone to visit her as she promised? [*Cassandro nods with his head*] She shouldn't have gone before I talked to you, and that's why I was looking for you. What did she do? Does she think she can cure her?
CASSANDRO: Eh, Lucrezio, you know well that only the person who got her into this situation can do that.
LUCREZIO: Are you referring to me? I don't think I've any deformity or any qualities to send a woman, to whom I'm betrothed, insane; neither do I know how I could have upset her so much.
CASSANDRO: You haven't upset her. You have pleased her far too much. It's because she wanted to please you that we've come to this.
LUCREZIO: Cassandro, I don't understand you.

CASSANDRO: You just don't want to understand. What need had you, Lucrezio, to make Lepida carry on like this?
LUCREZIO: Do you mean Lepida is putting on an act?
CASSANDRO: Didn't you know?
LUCREZIO: A girl like her putting on an act? There's something odd here.
CASSANDRO: There's nothing odd except what you started. What's the point, Lucrezio, of denying it? I know exactly how things are. If you loved her before and had an affair with her, it's certainly nothing to be proud of nor something which can go unnoticed. But you could have put everything right by marrying her. Why did you have to resort to such subterfuges?
LUCREZIO: I don't know whether I'm dreaming or awake. I've never made love to your daughter, and I never set eyes on her before the day you took me to see her. I can't understand what you're talking about.
CASSANDRO: If you wanted a bigger dowry, you should have thought of it before; this isn't the way to go about it. And if you did it to conceal her pregnancy and avoid my wrath, you should have considered that, since things had gone so far, I'd have forgiven you your mistake.
LUCREZIO: Is Lepida pregnant?
CASSANDRO: Well, you should know. After all it was you who did it.
LUCREZIO: *Me?* My God, what am I hearing!
CASSANDRO: Yes, you. She herself confessed to having been made pregnant by Lucrezio. You are Lucrezio, aren't you?
LUCREZIO: I wish I wasn't, with all these things I hear. Pregnant by me? Oh the lying, wicked girl! I give her back to you, I repudiate her, I leave her on your hands. Is this the sort of wife you're giving me? Pregnant by me? This is far worse than madness! Is this your way to bring a poor young man to his death?
CASSANDRO: This is the way to betray an honest man. He still persists in denying everything!
LUCREZIO: No more. I repudiate the bride, you and the whole marriage. So this is the way things are! I'm glad I found out in time. Let me go. [*Exit*]
CASSANDRO: [*Aside*] Either that rogue Targhetta has had the hide to play a trick in such an important matter, or this son-in-law of mine is the most two-faced man in the world. I don't know what to believe, what to do. Well, I'd better get back home right now.

SCENE IV

MESSER FEDERIGO, CASSANDRO

MESSER FEDERIGO: [*Aside*] Alas, what have I seen? What a scene have I had to witness! Oh treacherous tutor! Oh infamous Lepida! Giving yourself to a tutor!
CASSANDRO: [*Aside*] I'm dying to get home. I'll find out for myself how things are.
MESSER FEDERIGO: [*Aside*] I must learn to hate her as much as I loved her before; I shall plan to punish him and disappoint her. I must find the father at all costs and tell him everything.
CASSANDRO: [*Aside*] Either she'll tell me what sort of a trick this is or I'll cripple her. She can say what she likes but I won't increase her dowry.
MESSER FEDERIGO: [*Aside*] Oh Lepida, Lepida, you preferred a vile tutor to me! Have you chosen such a lover for yourself? You were feeding me leaves and keeping the fruits for this wicked man. Ah, there's Cassandro. I'll speak to him.
CASSANDRO: [*Aside*] What can this German want of me?
MESSER FEDERIGO: Messer Cassandro, I'm glad to have found you. I was born a gentleman and I have a gentleman's honour at heart; I hate those who don't show proper respect. I want to inform you of a great wrong which has been perpetrated in your house with dissimulation and treason.
CASSANDRO: [*Aside*] He's after me to repeat everything I've just learned from Targhetta. —Sir, I praise you for your fine spirit and thank you for your good deed. I already know that my daughter is putting on an act; but the ruse you may have heard about may not be true. And even if it were, given the identity of the person responsible, I'd do better to accept and put up with it.
MESSER FEDERIGO: What do you mean 'put up with it'? You obviously don't know everything. You're not the kind to put up with such an insult. Will you put up with the amorous talk, the immodest games and other more risqué things that they do together?
CASSANDRO: I certainly didn't know anything about this 'risqué' bit. I'll have to use force with her. Whether she likes it or not I've betrothed her to him and she'll be his wife.
MESSER FEDERIGO: Wife? You have betrothed your daughter to a tutor?

CASSANDRO: What do you mean 'tutor'? But you're a foreigner, and therefore you're ill-informed. Lucrezio, the husband of my daughter, is one of the most noble gentlemen of this city. What do you mean 'tutor'?

MESSER FEDERIGO: I can see that you don't understand me. I'll be open with you and reveal what I've just seen in your house.

CASSANDRO: [*Aside*] Alas, what else can there be? —Well, don't keep me waiting.

MESSER FEDERIGO: A while ago I was going to visit Messer Terenzio, as I do sometimes to learn something from him. First I was told that he had gone towards the garden. Then I found your servant in the courtyard. He said to me: "Go in through this door; he's gone upstairs" and he pointed to a little door behind which there is the winding staircase.[109]

CASSANDRO: [*Aside*] God help me. That door is never unlocked.

MESSER FEDERIGO: Without thinking twice I go up the stairs and I hear what sounds like whispering and the squeaking of a bed coming from a room. I stop and I slowly put my eye to the door which is ajar and I see your tutor on the bed embracing your daughter.

CASSANDRO: What? With my daughter?

MESSER FEDERIGO: Yes, sir.

CASSANDRO: On the bed with Lepida?

MESSER FEDERIGO: Exactly. I was dumbfounded at such a sight and I left quietly the same way I came without being seen or heard by anyone. And since this is a betrayal which cannot be endured, I was anxious to inform you despite the fact that Messer Terenzio was a good friend.

CASSANDRO: Wicked traitors! Are you sure you're not mistaken? And I always thought that man was so modest.

MESSER FEDERIGO: It's the modest ones you have to watch. I'm telling you I'm not mistaken. Why would I tell a lie?

CASSANDRO: You must be mistaken. It must have been her betrothed.

MESSER FEDERIGO: I don't know whether he's betrothed to her or not, but I know for sure that he's the tutor because I saw his face several times.

CASSANDRO: [*Aside*] Oh Lepida, what has this poor father of yours ever done to deserve such unhappiness in the few years that he's got left to live? I still can't believe it.

MESSER FEDERIGO: You're still in time to go and find out for yourself since they're probably still at it.

CASSANDRO: Yes, I must find out. Let's go. I'd like you with me just in case I need some help. If I find that things are the way you say, I shall have to do something about it.
MESSER FEDERIGO: I'll be happy to come, I'm obliged to, out of compassion for you and because of the gravity of the situation. Let's try to proceed without making any noise. Otherwise they'll hear us and run away. Come this way. Let me lead you.
CASSANDRO: As you like, let's go. Oh, how I have been disgraced! How miserable I feel! [*Exeunt*]

SCENE V

VIOLANTE, GIGLIETTA

VIOLANTE: [*In the street*] Giglietta, Giglietta?
GIGLIETTA: [*Upstairs*] Who's calling me?
VIOLANTE: Come to the window.
GIGLIETTA: What do you want from me in such a hurry?
VIOLANTE: I'd like your help because I'm in a bit of a spot.
GIGLIETTA: What now?
VIOLANTE: The pilgrim, poor girl, is sick. She's come home half dead and she's fainted. I've tried for a while to make her come to but with no success. I'd like you to come down too.
GIGLIETTA: Poor girl, I'm sorry for her. I'd be happy to come but, as you know, I can't very well leave this girl on her own.
VIOLANTE: What do you think would happen if you left her alone for a while?
GIGLIETTA: I wouldn't leave her under any circumstances; right now her condition is making her do strange things—such strange things! I couldn't leave her now they're reaching a climax.[110]
VIOLANTE: Tell me at least what you think I should do.
GIGLIETTA: If she's fainted, you should know. Sprinkle rose water, rub her wrists, loosen her clothes.
VIOLANTE: I've done all that but to no avail. I tell you, her male companion and her female servant, the one who's sick, are desperate.
GIGLIETTA: Perhaps she's pregnant and that's making her sick. Don't you know what to do in such cases?
VIOLANTE: Not me, since I've always managed to avoid such a situation.

GIGLIETTA: Is she talking at all? Isn't she saying what she feels, where it hurts?
VIOLANTE: She didn't say a word for a long while; then she sighed heavily and said: "Ah, treacherous Lucrezio!" I suspect that your Lucrezio, with the excuse of taking her to cure his wife, has done something awful to her.
GIGLIETTA: How could he? He wasn't at home when she came and, besides, wasn't she with her male companion?
VIOLANTE: I don't know about that. What did her words mean? All of a sudden she's run down and almost lifeless.
GIGLIETTA: Have you touched her to see if she's sweating?
VIOLANTE: She's not sweating at all; on the contrary, she's as cold as ice. What beautiful skin she has, Giglietta!
GIGLIETTA: Try to soothe her stomach with some application, and keep her warm. I'll rush over there the moment somebody comes home. Oh dear, I hear such a commotion inside! God help, what can it be?
VIOLANTE: It must be Lepida carrying on in her usual fashion.
GIGLIETTA: [*Aside*] I can hear the old man screaming. Poor me, those poor lovers! How did he get in without me seeing him? I certainly kept a good watch! —Violante, I must run.
VIOLANTE: [*Aside*] I haven't managed to get anything from her to help this poor girl. Poor dear! She knows so many remedies that she uses to help others, and now she can't help herself. What a situation! Inn-keepers, ferrymen, publicans don't usually grow attached to anyone. But I've got so fond of this woman now that I suffer for her. These Spanish women are certainly attractive. I'll go and see what she's doing. I'd like to help her the best way I can. [*Exit*]

SCENE VI

MESSER FEDERIGO, CASSANDRO

MESSER FEDERIGO: Are you satisfied now, Messer Cassandro?
CASSANDRO: I wish I was blind and dead. Treacherous tutor! Wicked daughter! How much better it would have been if you had really been a simpleton! And you have indeed been mad since you went out of your mind when you decided to do such a wicked deed. Let other fathers learn what it means to employ young people in the

house. Let them not be fooled by those who appear to be modest, for they turn out to be devils disguised as angels. Ah, poor me! I have so many reasons to complain: my daughter's treachery, his deceit, Giglietta's betrayal—since she must have had a hand in all this! What will you do Cassandro? What decision will you make? You counsel me, sir, since anger and hurt stop me from thinking straight.

MESSER FEDERIGO: I almost regret having revealed this thing to you. Though I could have foreseen how much you'd have been grieved, and rightly so, nevertheless now that I see you suffer, I'd like to have nothing to do with the situation, especially since you might be angry with me from now on.

CASSANDRO: How could I be angry with you? Don't say that. On the contrary, I'm grateful to you.

MESSER FEDERIGO: Back home, in Germany, these dishonest actions are abominated by everyone, and everyone thinks it honourable to make them public so that the culprits can be punished. I can't tell you how indignant I am about all this, and not just because I've great compassion for you.

CASSANDRO: I can tell that from the generous person you have shown yourself to be, and if this situation makes you indignant, think of what it does to me. I'm resolved to take revenge at all costs: I don't want them to go unpunished. As for my daughter, I know already what I've to do. I want her to end her life inside the walls of a nunnery—not just as an ordinary nun,[111] but as a nun under the strictest discipline of all! But I haven't decided yet what to do with that wicked, iniquitous man; I'd like to punish him as best I can. What would you suggest?

MESSER FEDERIGO: We must hustle him out of this world. He deserves no lesser punishment. But to keep things quiet, I'd suggest locking him up in that room, where we've left him, until nightfall. Tonight, I'd put him in a bag and I'd throw him into the Arno. Leave this to me, I'd like to take care of this matter.

CASSANDRO: Thank you for being so eager to help, but these are dangerous actions. If this were to become public it'd be the downfall of me and my family.

MESSER FEDERIGO: You're right. What made me talk like that was my regard for you.

CASSANDRO: Believe me, I'm truly concerned about my honour. But should we be caught carrying out this crime, which couldn't be kept hidden for too long, I'd run the risk of losing everything and of compromising my honour as well. So perhaps it would be better to punish him by surrendering him to the law; I surely couldn't be disgraced by that. It wouldn't be the first time that an honourable gentleman like me has had to suffer these acts of violence through no fault of his own.

MESSER FEDERIGO: Well spoken! But this foolish world sometimes takes the wrong view in the most important matters.

CASSANDRO: Let it take what view it wishes. A wise man mustn't be swayed by the judgement of the ignorant populace. I intend to throw myself at the feet of the prince and tell him all about this treachery. He is justice in person and in these cases he's very strict.

MESSER FEDERIGO: Very strict indeed, from what I've heard. Then since you've decided this line of action, there is no time to waste; I'd like to come with you, if you'll let me.

CASSANDRO: All right, then, let's go. Just look at the circumstances in which I've to avail myself of our prince's goodness and justice! What happiness I have derived from my only daughter! Oh, Lepida, how joyless now appears the hour in which I begot you! Are these the delights which you bestow on your father? Are these the fruits of my labour? Are these the rewards for my love and care? I'll make you pay for this, and I'll also punish that wretched Giglietta who must have been the cause of all this evil. I wanted to catch them unawares and I was planning to have that traitor caught without him suspecting anything, but they heard us and we had to reveal ourselves.

MESSER FEDERIGO: If I hadn't been with you, he'd have certainly escaped.

CASSANDRO: That's certain; but now he's locked up and he won't escape. And it was a good idea to lock the back door too, just to make sure. I think I'll bolt it as well. Let's go this way; we'll get there more quickly.

MESSER FEDERIGO: Let's go. [*Exeunt*]

ACT V

SCENE I

GIGLIETTA, TARGHETTA

GIGLIETTA: [*Upstairs*] What will you do, Giglietta? Everything is locked up front and back. Poor me. If only someone would come by and unbolt this door for me! I'd like to run away. God knows how I hate leaving those two poor youngsters locked up in there. But since I can't help them, I might as well help myself. I'd better go away and take my savings with me. How unfortunate I am. In that very room I've left four pounds of tow which was the stuffing of the canvas for my towels, and now I don't even have a rag to my name. No matter where I look I can't see anybody coming.

TARGHETTA: [*In the street*] I've got to find this German at all costs; but perhaps I'm no longer in time to warn him. Something is bound to go wrong today. He was seen with my master not long ago. What on earth was he doing with him? Are Germans becoming so sly that they befriend the parents of the girls they love?

GIGLIETTA: [*Upstairs*] I think I can see somebody coming this way. If I'm not mistaken it's Targhetta coming home. If he can unbolt the door then I'll shoot off. I hope he doesn't turn off beforehand!

TARGHETTA: [*In the street*] I wonder what this means.

GIGLIETTA: [*Upstairs*] Look how slowly he's coming—Hurry up, Targhetta, you're wanted at home. Hurry up.

TARGHETTA: Coming. Why all the hurry?

GIGLIETTA: Hurry up! Everything's in a dreadful mess.

TARGHETTA: [*Aside*] I hope that German hasn't been unlucky enough to be caught! —Hey, this door's locked! What does this mean? Who bolted it from the outside?

GIGLIETTA: Open up and come up here and you'll know why.

TARGHETTA: [*Aside*] I'm sure Messer Federigo must have been discovered in the house and the old man must have locked him inside. When I heard they'd been seen together I thought my leg was being pulled, but my informant must really have known what was going on. If that's so, I'm ruined—Was it the master who bolted this door, Giglietta?
GIGLIETTA: You're infuriating! Why don't you open up and come inside?
TARGHETTA: [*Aside*] Here's the master. And he's actually with Messer Federigo. But what's that police officer doing with them? I'd better stay hidden! Before I show up I want to know how things stand. [*Exit*]
GIGLIETTA: Where are you going, you rogue? [*Aside*] He's gone. Here's the old man with some other people. I'm done for, there's no way out. This is my downfall! [*Withdraws from the window*]

SCENE II

OFFICER, CASSANDRO, MESSER FEDERIGO

OFFICER: There's no need for you to speak to the Prince. You should be satisfied with what the Lord Commissioner[112] told you: if this man confesses, or if you can get clear proof of his action in any other way without a long enquiry, he'll send him to jail.
CASSANDRO: He can't deny the deed since I caught him red-handed. This gentleman can witness that.
OFFICER: That will be enough. In cases where a father accuses his own daughter, especially a father of your standing, and especially when it concerns private matters, we always believe the evidence given by one reliable witness. If this is not enough, there's always another way of obtaining the truth.
MESSER FEDERIGO: Such as?
OFFICER: Torture.
CASSANDRO: In all these proceedings I want you to act quickly so that I can get rid of him without too much fuss. And if it's possible I'd like it to be made known that he's accused of theft.
MESSER FEDERIGO: You can say that again. He's robbed you of a most precious thing—your honour.
OFFICER: I'm sure that the Lord Commissioner will agree to that. And you can be assured that, if he's convicted, by tomorrow evening

at the latest he'll be sent to row in a galley.¹¹³ His Highness¹¹⁴ has issued some very stern decrees against rape and adultery. In such cases he has the authority to enforce and inflict severe and speedy punishment. I could give you a dozen examples of the severity of our lords in such cases. They don't exempt anyone, whether they're noblemen or members of religious orders or courtiers.

CASSANDRO: Captain, we must act quickly before the Chancellor of the University hears of this; he might want to place the matter under his jurisdiction since a university student is involved.

MESSER FEDERIGO: What university student? Tutors aren't students, nor do they enjoy the same privileges.¹¹⁵

OFFICER: And besides, the Chancellor can't interfere in such an important matter.

CASSANDRO: Come in, this is my house.

OFFICER: Lead the way.

CASSANDRO: Come. [*Enter Cassandro's house*]

SCENE III

CAVICCHIA, CARLETTO

CAVICCHIA: This must be one of those days in which no one can find anything. Each one of us is looking for his master and neither of us can find him.

CARLETTO: What's worse in my case is that my master has made me think today. And that's the least of my troubles. What I'm worried about is that he may be occupied in some problem that will have made him forget about eating. I bet he's gone to distract himself at the Guadagni household,¹¹⁶ talking about the latest news from France and Belgium.¹¹⁷ I really don't know where to look for him.

CAVICCHIA: My master's probably gossiping with some German about his emperor: whether he's made a truce with the Turks, and similar idiocies. The other day he was saying he'd have liked to be at some Diet or other.¹¹⁸ I told him that as long as I was in his service I didn't want to diet: diets are only good for those who suffer from intestinal catarrh or syphilis. What do we care, when we're miles away, what people do in countries which are so far off? A really important piece of news would be that Pinsucchia, the innkeeper, has opened a new barrel of muscatel or that Tartaglia has roasted a large suckling calf and that there are lots of partridges

and pheasants about. Plague on those who trouble themselves about irrelevant matters.
CARLETTO: You sound very much like Targhetta whom I saw not long ago. You're two kindred spirits—each of you thinks only of his stomach.
CAVICCHIA: Targhetta is a real gent and we're old friends. If you heard him talk of food and wine and saw how knowledgeable he is about it, you'd think you were talking to Solomon in person.[119] Hear this. Last Sunday, when we were about to go to church, he was complaining about how badly our masters divided up the time set aside for our bodily pleasures. Sometimes, he was saying, they spend four or five hours listening to world news, to music, and to stories, and as much time looking at medals, studying paintings, watching plays, gaping at some woman—all things which aren't worth a cent. They also want to devote time to their noses and they'll spend three hours in a perfume shop sniffing waters, oils, powders, scenting their gloves and other similar stupidities. They don't even devote one hour in the whole day to the mouth, the source of life. But Targhetta talks about it all the time. When I listen to him, I'm really impressed. Aren't you?
CARLETTO: Ha, ha, I see; he'd like to spend as much time at the table as in bed, and divide his life between eating and sleeping. I can see that you've found your Solomon. But you've been luckier than him since your master is a German.
CAVICCHIA: That'd be true if we hadn't ended up in this boarding house. A real dump.
CARLETTO: That's not true; Violante really looks after the place.
CAVICCHIA: How can she, if she's always overbooking? Do you know who's a good innkeeper? The one who gives lodgings to only a few clients. You praise Violante because she's an old friend of yours. When you send her a protegé she tries harder to please him. I know these things because I've never had there a perfect glass of wine that I could drink with all my five senses.
CARLETTO: You make me laugh and today I really don't feel like it. Drink with all your five senses? That's really funny! Ha, ha!
CAVICCHIA: Listen and then you can laugh. As for taste, as you know, you must taste the wine and find it pleasant, mellow, pungent; it must leave your lips dry. The eye must play its part in seeing that the wine is clear, sparkling, and has a good colouring. What's the use of having a wine which has the best taste in the world but

is cloudy and colourless? The nose also has to be satisfied since a good wine, when you smell it, must have a certain bouquet, a scent of violets, an aroma which refreshes you. If it smelled of mould or of wood, you wouldn't like it. And if the wine isn't cool, especially in summer, and, when you touch it with the lips, you can feel that it is warm or lukewarm, how could you ever drink it?

CARLETTO: You're doing fine so far. But I want to see how you take care of the hearing: unless you shake your glass, I can't see what other noise you can hear.

CAVICCHIA: Listen hard, because this is more important than you think. If you're given a glass of wine in your hand and you're told this is Greco, Panzano, Portercole or Chianti,[120] doesn't the sound of these sweet words make you drink with greater pleasure? If you hear that it's a wine from Posticcia,[121] or wine grown on the plains or vin brulé, wouldn't you feel put off?

CARLETTO: My word, that's really a good one! You must have got it from Targhetta. If I listened to you I'd waste a lot of time, since you seem to be less interested in finding your master than I am in finding mine. I'm off now.

CAVICCHIA: Wait for me; I'd like to come with you. [*Exeunt*]

SCENE IV

CASSANDRO, MESSER FEDERIGO, OFFICER,
MESSER TERENZIO, PILGRIM, RICCIARDO

CASSANDRO: Stay away from me, away from me, you traitor, you rapacious wolf in sheep's clothing who devours people's honour.

MESSER FEDERIGO: Insolent tutor, traitor, are these the subjects, is this the behaviour you teach in a nobleman's house? And you wanted to wriggle out of it by offering marriage!

OFFICER: Leave this to me. Every sinner sooner or later gets what he deserves.

MESSER TERENZIO: [*In fetters*] I put up with your insults patiently because you are her father, just as I also put up with this officer because he's doing his duty as law enforcer. But I can't accept being insulted by someone who has accused me out of envy and who has perhaps tried to do exactly what I've done.

MESSER FEDERIGO: Shut up, you lying coward.

MESSER TERENZIO: It's cowardly to insult someone who can't defend himself.
CASSANDRO: How dare you, traitor? Is this the way you repay me for the trust I placed in you?
MESSER TERENZIO: Messer Cassandro, what I've done I've done not as a traitor but as a lover driven by that same reason which has so many times driven, and still drives, very learned men and men with noble and generous spirits. If you, however, see things differently because of your anger, I beg you at least to forgive Lepida; only her naivety and my insistence have made her a party to this. Take all your revenge out on me, me alone, and forgive her.
CASSANDRO: As for you, death is too good a punishment. As for Lepida, I know well enough what to do with her.
MESSER TERENZIO: At least, out of Christian charity and considering that she's pregnant, don't be so hard on her that you endanger an innocent creature who's your own flesh and blood.
CASSANDRO: What blood, you wicked man? I'll never recognize as mine this eternal reminder of my disgrace! I'd rather smash it to pieces against the wall with my own hands. That's enough, now. Take him away and report his confession to the Lord Commissioner.
OFFICER: It shall be done. But at least let him get fully dressed. He's only wearing his light vest.
MESSER FEDERIGO: I'll go and fetch his fur coat from his room. [*Exit*]
PILGRIM: [*Approaching*] Get things ready to leave tomorrow. I hate this place so much that it's like hell to me. But first I want to go and confront that wicked, treacherous man for the last time. I want to reproach him for his wrongdoing.
RICCIARDO: You've hardly recovered from the fainting fit you suffered a little while ago, and you want to go gadding about. Do as I say: rest now, and leave Pisa without ever talking to him again; I can just see it now, he'll try to deceive you again with his treacherous words.
PILGRIM: No, never. Now his trickery stares me in the face and I know the man is a traitor. I must reveal myself to him; if I didn't confront him with my virtuous behaviour and his treachery I wouldn't have anything to appease my desperation.
RICCIARDO: Let me, at least, come with you.
PILGRIM: No, I want to be alone so that I can talk to him more freely. Return home.

RICCIARDO: I obey you, but unwillingly. [*Exit*]
PILGRIM: [*Aside*] There's no need to think back to Theseus or Bireno:[122] this is a worse betrayal than theirs. Ah, why does old Cassandro have that man in fetters? I must get closer.
CASSANDRO: [*Aside*] He can't have been able to find the coat.
PILGRIM: Messer Cassandro, I was glad to learn that it was a pretence and that we don't have to trouble with a cure.
CASSANDRO: Alas, unfortunately too many truths have been uncovered! This wicked man whom you see here is the cause of all the trouble.
PILGRIM: How?
CASSANDRO: If you can wait until I've got him off my hands, I'll tell you how things are; I owe you too much not to reveal everything to you.
PILGRIM: I'm looking forward to hearing it. [*Aside*] What could it have been? I'd like to find out before I talk to Lucrezio.
MESSER FEDERIGO: [*Returns*] Here's your coat.
OFFICER: Give it to me; help me put it on.
MESSER TERENZIO: How obstinately Fortuna is set against me!
CASSANDRO: Send this wicked man to row in the galley.
MESSER FEDERIGO: Yes, send him to study at a bench[123] that's worthy of his intellect, and place in his hand a pen dipped in the kind of ink he deserves.
OFFICER: Don't upset yourself anymore; tomorrow, at the latest, he'll be assigned to a galley.
MESSER TERENZIO: What, to a galley? I'd rather you killed me. And even if you don't want to do it out of benevolence towards me, do it for your daughter. While she's my wife, she won't be able to marry again. If you make me die, as I implore you, you'll end my miseries and set her free.
CASSANDRO: You still insist on using the word 'wife'? What effrontery!
OFFICER: Careful. If they're really husband and wife, then the police can't intervene.
CASSANDRO: What husband and wife? This is something that he has made up to complicate matters.
MESSER FEDERIGO: And besides, these secret weddings aren't approved by the Council.[124]
CASSANDRO: You, you claim that my daughter is your wife?
OFFICER: Come, let's go.

MESSER TERENZIO: Good Lord! A man of my standing in jail where wicked and base people are sent!
MESSER FEDERIGO: Look here, tutor! Who do you think you are?
MESSER TERENZIO: What an unlucky destiny! Wasn't it better for me to remain a slave in the hands of the Turks rather than be ransomed, freed and now led to such an awful and shameful punishment?
MESSER FEDERIGO: So you escaped from the Turks' hands and perhaps from prison to come and contaminate the houses of gentlemen? You scoundrel! Go back to what you deserve.
MESSER TERENZIO: Oh, if only the Ormanni[125] could see how a member of their family is being tortured and insulted today!
MESSER FEDERIGO: [Aside] What can this man have to do with the Ormanni?
MESSER TERENZIO: Oh my family, oh my dear brothers. Is this the hope that I entertained, after so many hazards, of seeing you again in Vienna?
MESSER FEDERIGO: [Aside] Vienna, the Ormanni, a slave in the hands of the Turks. . . . My God, if this were perchance the person whom I love so much, to whom I am drawn! Let me ask him. —Tell me now . . .
CASSANDRO: Let him go; we've wasted too much time here. Come on, take away this scoundrel.
MESSER FEDERIGO: Please, Messer Cassandro, be patient until I can explain to myself this feeling I have. Who knows? Today you may be able to rid yourself of all your troubles! [To Messer Terenzio] Which Vienna, which Ormanni are you talking about? What have you got to do with them?
MESSER TERENZIO: Now I should tell you immediately who I really am, so that you and Messer Cassandro can know how wrong you are to insult me the way you do. But what's the point of doing it in a place where no one can verify the truth of what I say and where no one knows anything about my family?
MESSER FEDERIGO: Just imagine that there was someone here who knew this family and Vienna very well, what would you have to say?
MESSER TERENZIO: I'd say that I'm the son of Daniele Ormanno and that should be enough to guarantee my nobility.
MESSER FEDERIGO: [Aside] But I too am the son of Daniele Ormanno. This must be my brother. Alas, I've placed a person whom I loved so much and yearned for so much in such danger! But

he might be tricking me. I need to find out a bit more—If it's true that you're Daniele Ormanno's son, then you're the son of a nobleman indeed. Now tell me, when and why did you leave him?

MESSER TERENZIO: I never really did leave him; twelve years ago, while I was staying with him at a villa far from Vienna, I was taken prisoner during a raid by the Turks who assaulted suddenly one night.

CASSANDRO: I'm waiting to see where all this talk is leading to. I hope, captain, that you don't mind waiting a while.

OFFICER: Not at all. I, too, am interested in hearing this story.

MESSER FEDERIGO: What's the name of the villa where you were kidnapped?

MESSER TERENZIO: Its name is Villa Roveta, a very well known villa in that area.

MESSER FEDERIGO: [*Aside*] My God, what am I destined to experience today! —Did your father have any other children besides you?

MESSER TERENZIO: Two younger ones: a baby and another one almost my age who's called Federigo. If he were here and could see what a state his brother is in, he'd obtain some favour, demand some respect for me. And because of the well-known nobility of our family, I'm sure he'd get it.

MESSER FEDERIGO: [*Aside*] Everything would match except for his name—I know this Daniele and all his family very well but I don't recall him having a son called Terenzio.

MESSER TERENZIO: It's true and my name is not Terenzio; I took this name when I came to this house and posed as a tutor since I didn't want to reveal my true identity while exercising such a lowly profession. My real name is Lucrezio.

MESSER FEDERIGO: Oh Lucrezio, brother! I'm your Federigo.

MESSER TERENZIO: You're Federigo, my brother? I hug you with my heart since I can't do it with my arms.

CASSANDRO: Lucrezio, ha, ha. Now I understand why the pretence had been organized at Lucrezio's instigation.

PILGRIM: [*Aside*] Good Lord! this means that my Lucrezio isn't as guilty as I thought.

MESSER TERENZIO: But why do you say that you are from Spruch[126] and call yourself Alberghetti?

MESSER FEDERIGO: I'll tell you. But I can't stand seeing you tied up like this. Messer Cassandro, please, let him be untied for a little

while at least.
OFFICER: I'd prefer to do as he asks, Messer Cassandro, since this very gentleman tied him up.
CASSANDRO: Untie him; I'd do a greater favour than this for Messer Federigo.
MESSER FEDERIGO: You must know that Messer Guglielmo Alberghetti from Spruch, a gentleman who became a very close friend of our father after you were taken away, had no children. Since he loved me very much, he asked, and was granted by our father, the right to adopt me as his son. He gave me the surname Alberghetti and as such, and with Spruch as my home town, I'm known and called. This is to my advantage in Pisa as I enjoy life at the court and have the favour of His Highness.
CASSANDRO: Watch out, Messer Federigo, don't be duped. This man has always maintained he came from the Marche region and, in fact, he speaks Italian as well as we do.
MESSER TERENZIO: That's nothing to be surprised about; during the eleven years that I lived as a slave in Rhodes up to the moment when I was freed last year, I was always with other Italian slaves, all people of a certain standing. Talking to them helped me not only to learn Italian but also not to forget Latin which I had learnt in Vienna. When I came to this house I pretended to come from the Marche region to add plausibility to the story that I was a tutor.
MESSER FEDERIGO: Oh brother, how much misfortune I've caused you! Without knowing it, I've betrayed my own blood! Messer Cassandro, you are wise and generous; by forgiving my brother you can also save your honour and I think that you won't be unsympathetic to what I'm about to say. You've already heard from us—and you can get further confirmation—of the nobility of our family, and we haven't even spoken yet of its wealth. Therefore, it would be an action worthy of a person like you to accept and give your agreement to what these two say they have done in all secrecy.
CASSANDRO: Only the person who has been offended knows how sweet revenge is and how ardently he yearns for it. The injury I have sustained is too great to be dismissed so lightly.
MESSER FEDERIGO: The injury perpetrated by a man motivated by love is never great. To cancel these mistakes from the face of the earth would be equivalent to erasing youth from it.

CASSANDRO: Messer Federigo, when you weren't involved in this matter you considered it an ugly affair, and you yourself were urging me on to seek punishment.

MESSER FEDERIGO: I did so because I thought that the action had been carried out by an infamous tutor and I didn't see any way of settling the matter honourably. Now I deem it worthy of your pardon because it was carried out by a noble person; now it's easy for you to preserve your honour and save him great shame.

MESSER TERENZIO: God is my witness when I say that I had no other intention but to take Lepida as my lawful wife, hoping that, once I could reveal my real identity, she wouldn't be denied to me. Her madness was feigned for no other reason but to put off the other wedding. But if you can't be moved to pardon me, Messer Cassandro, make me suffer as much as you like: I'll still love and respect you as much as I'll love your daughter for ever. Do as you please with me.

MESSER FEDERIGO: Is it possible, Messer Cassandro, that you're still unmoved? [*Kneels at Cassandro's feet*] For God's sake I implore your pity: if you don't want to free my brother, if you don't want to accept him into your household and give him to your daughter, give him to me at least since it was I who surrendered him into your hands.

CASSANDRO: Please get up.

MESSER FEDERIGO: I won't move from your feet as long as you are angry and withhold your forgiveness.

PILGRIM: Man is closest to resembling God when he forgives. Moreover, one should look after one's interests. The reasons brought forward by these two brothers seem very compelling.

CASSANDRO: I certainly won't forgive him unless he marries her. But how can that be if she's already married to somebody else?

PILGRIM: Lucrezio, if I've understood correctly, hasn't given her the ring yet and now, when he hears of this, there is no way he'd ever marry her. If he were here, I'm certain that he'd beg you to give her to Messer Terenzio.

CASSANDRO: Well, since this is how things are, I willingly forgive him. I accept him and embrace him as a son and as a son-in-law, granting him Lepida as his wife with the same dowry I had promised the other Lucrezio.

MESSER FEDERIGO: Oh Messer Cassandro, how deeply I'm indebted to you!

MESSER TERENZIO: Oh my kind father! For I really ought to call you my real father rather than father-in-law.

CASSANDRO: Captain, I want you to rejoice with us as well. Now that things have turned out in such a way, no legal infringement has been committed.

OFFICER: You're right; I've heard and seen everything with great pleasure.

CASSANDRO: Please take this out of love for me and as a reward for your troubles. [*Hands the officer some money*]

OFFICER: Thank you kindly. May God grant you every joy!

MESSER TERENZIO: Oh, my loving brother, I've found you again at last. I want to embrace you again: I'll never have my fill of this.

MESSER FEDERIGO: How could you, Lucrezio, stop yourself from coming straight home, after being freed from the Turks, to make your family happy?

MESSER TERENZIO: A very rich Palermitan merchant, on his way from Alexandria, stopped by chance in Rhodes and, moved by Christian piety, freed me and three other Italian slaves with his own money. I agreed to go with him to Palermo and I liked his gentle manners so much that I couldn't detach myself from him for four months; in the meantime, though I tried repeatedly to send news of myself to our father, I never got an answer. Tell me, Federigo, what news do you have of our family? Is father still alive?

MESSER FEDERIGO: Yes, thank God, but tell me . . .

CASSANDRO: You'll have all the time you want to talk about your respective adventures. Come on. I'm dying to get back home.

PILGRIM: Go and console the young girl; she must be in a terrible state. I couldn't tell you, Messer Cassandro, how happy I am about all this.

CASSANDRO: Thank you very much! I absolutely insist that you come to the wedding.

PILGRIM: I can't come now but, before I leave, I certainly will come and congratulate your daughter.

CASSANDRO: Let's go upstairs.

MESSER TERENZIO: I came down these stairs, not long ago, grieving and in pain. Now I climb up with great joy. Oh Fortuna, I forgive you for all my past injuries since with one stroke you have raised me from so much misery to such happiness.

MESSER FEDERIGO: Let's go, let's go.

[*Exeunt, except for the Pilgrim*]

SCENE V

PILGRIM alone

What strange things fate has in store for us! How wonderfully sometimes difficult situations are resolved! The man who was considered to be the most unhappy, now finds himself to be the happiest. I, who thought I had reason to complain of Lucrezio, have discovered that I was treating him unjustly only because I had mistaken another of the same name for him. But how can this help me free myself of my passion? It only makes me shift my suspicions from one thing to another since I now start doubting everyone and I don't know where to stop: now I'm worse off. Certainly he must have taken up with another woman, since I heard this morning from his very mouth that it was because of his love for another woman that he didn't want to marry this one. Ah, Lucrezio, if this isn't the case, how else can I explain how you've forgotten your Drusilla? If I'm not mistaken, if your actions, your words and your tears were not deceitful, surely I was securely lodged in your heart when you left me. What other proof do you need to be convinced besides the fact that he never returned after having pledged to do so? What will you do, Drusilla? Will you give vent to your resentment of him, as you planned? But I can't do this without revealing myself to him. You'd be mad to do so because, since he has forgotten you, he would disdain you and thus add insult to injury. What will you do, then? Here he comes. Shall I go or shall I talk to him? Alas, my heart is failing me. On one side I feel that I should avoid him, but on the other I feel I should talk to him. He approaches. I must make up my mind. I shall talk to him—without revealing myself—I want to sound him out and I'll behave according to the way he reacts. Oh, Lucrezio, if only you were as faithful as you're handsome I'd be happy!

SCENE VI

LUCREZIO, PILGRIM

LUCREZIO: [*Aside*] How wretched and ill-treated I am. I've been given a pregnant wife. If I find Taddeo Pacifico, who was the

go-between, I shall tell him off so sharply that he won't want to arrange marriages again.
PILGRIM: [*Aside*] He's talking to himself and seems very worried. Oh God, I have no courage.
LUCREZIO: [*Aside*] How insistent that old man was in claiming that it was me! What a diabolical woman! She has feigned it all to cover up her wrongdoings and then blames me for it!
PILGRIM: [*Aside*] Drusilla, you're a coward; you must gather courage.
LUCREZIO: [*Aside*] Alas, what a mess I got myself into! And I'm afraid I've gotten the pilgrim into the fray on my account as well. Luckily here she comes. —I'm glad, madam, to have found you. I'm sorry if you have encountered trouble for my sake concerning the matter for which I consulted you this morning. Things have turned out in such a way that one would only get a painful headache from being involved. They have accused me of such strange things.
PILGRIM: I know very well what you mean, but after you've learnt what I recently found out you'll feel somewhat relieved. For that reason I wanted to see you, because from the moment I met you I liked your looks and your manners and you've made me feel sorry for you.
LUCREZIO: I'm greatly indebted to you, madam. Tell me, please, what you've heard.
PILGRIM: I will. But first of all I want you to know that all your troubles are a punishment for something you've done and you won't ever get rid of your difficulties until you've repented and made amends.
LUCREZIO: I'm frail, as all other human beings are, and I could have committed many errors; though I don't know for which particular one I'm being punished. Since you do, however, please tell me so that I can make amends if there's still time.
PILGRIM: The punishment meted out by God is often related to the type of sin committed; therefore, the fact you've been deceived over this wife suggests—please ask yourself if, by chance, this may be so—that you, in turn, have deceived some other woman.
LUCREZIO: As I said, I could have committed many errors but I've never deceived any woman: I'm certain of this because I would never have committed such an infamy.
PILGRIM: Watch what you're saying. Haven't you ever loved a woman?
LUCREZIO: Alas, yes; I've loved one woman and one alone and I shall

never love any other for as long as I remember her and I'm alive.
PILGRIM: Did she live in this city?
LUCREZIO: No, madam, she's from a faraway place.
PILGRIM: [*Aside*] If God could only help me some more! —Which place, if it's not too presumtuous of me to ask?
LUCREZIO: You presumptuous? I accept all this as a sign of your affection. She lived in one of the major cities in Spain.
PILGRIM: [*Aside*] This could still turn out a happy day for me. —How could you love this woman if you had already decided to marry this Lepida? This shows that you had forgotten her love. How do you expect God to free you of this pain now since you're not only unwilling to atone for the past but you're even reluctant to come out with it?
LUCREZIO: I can't very well confess to have failed in something which, in all my conscience, I believe I carried out as I should.
PILGRIM: What do you mean? Should you have left the woman you loved so much for another one? Don't hide anything from me since I am only too well acquainted with the circumstances and with the young woman involved.
LUCREZIO: There's nothing I wish more than for you to know everything in detail; that way you'll see clearly that I'm innocent.
PILGRIM: Innocent, you say? And how can one be innocent when one breaks a pledge and abandons the beloved? And what reason did she give to cause all this? Was it perhaps that she didn't love you more than her own life? Was it perhaps because you found her unchaste? You yourself, who meant everything to her, know that only very small favours were conceded to you. And with what difficulty! Was it perhaps that she gave you reason to feel jealous because she talked to some other suitor? Wasn't she held in high regard, well thought of by everyone in the city, and considered to be among the best of women? Wasn't the very decision of taking you, a foreigner, as a husband instead of one of the many local men who sought her (and she did this behind her uncle's back), enough to bind you two for ever? And instead you, full of deceit, the moment you're back in Pisa, get married again and you forget you left a wife back in Valencia. You were about to entertain yourself with her while the other poor woman, full of love and loyalty, was waiting in vain for your return. Don't you consider this a dreadful betrayal, which deserves severe punishment from divine justice?

LUCREZIO: I'm astonished! On the one hand you know how things went just as if you had been there, but on the other you're not at all aware of the final outcome. It's true that Drusilla loved me. It's true that she was a rare and divine creature. It's true that she did things which made me indebted to her for ever, and I'll always feel so towards that blessed spirit. But what have I done wrong? Let myself be persuaded to marry again after her death? Nothing else could have taken her away from me. Drusilla, blessed soul, you can see from heaven whether I've done wrong or not; you know that, while you were alive, you were the mistress of my heart and you took it with you.

PILGRIM: Don't cry Lucrezio. You've no reason to cry, even if you think you do. If you must cry, cry because of your negligence and your carelessness in trying to ascertain the state of things which are really important to you. You say that Drusilla is dead. How can you be sure of it? Were you there?

LUCREZIO: No, I wasn't. But a close friend of mine from Lucca was, and he gave me the painful news.

PILGRIM: Did you have to accept only one report of something which took place so far away? If she was so dear to you and you to her, as you are claiming, why didn't you seek confirmation through other sources? Why didn't you go straight away to wash those bones with your tears?

LUCREZIO: I thought of doing that many times. But I didn't because, once there, I would have aroused suspicions and cast doubts on her integrity with all my lamentations. There was nothing further to find out about her death, since my friend from Lucca had seen her on a bier. Please, let's not open this wound again since it renews my suffering too much. Tell me now what you had to say and allay some of my present suffering, since all else is mundane and transitory by comparison with the eternal loss of my Drusilla.

PILGRIM: Why eternal? Perhaps Drusilla is not dead; perhaps she's alive!

LUCREZIO: I know she lives in heaven: I'm sure of that because of her divine qualities and angelic virtue.

PILGRIM: I'm telling you she may be alive on earth. I doubt, however, whether time, which effaces all memories, hasn't erased her image from your heart.

LUCREZIO: How could that be? Every day that passes I love her even more, and when I compare her with other women I recognize that

she was the queen of them all. How could she be erased from my heart? I tell you this much: if by dying I could bring Drusilla back to life, I'd find death the sweetest thing.
PILGRIM: [*Aside*] How fortunate I am!
LUCREZIO: It's useless, however, to think about impossible things. Fortuna planned to show me such wealth and then, by taking it away, make me the most sorrowful man on earth.
PILGRIM: If it's true that she loved you as much as you say she did, then certainly you're justified in remembering her so lovingly. But if she were alive, do you think she'd feel towards you as she did in the past, after you neglected to make certain whether she was dead or not?
LUCREZIO: If only she were alive I could put up with anything. Even if she thought I had erred by trusting the testimony of a friend, I'd hope to find forgiveness from her kind heart, since she'd see that my love not only hasn't diminished but has grown fonder.
PILGRIM: If then she were alive, would you feel towards her as you once did? Would you be loyal to her?
LUCREZIO: If she were alive I'd want her as my wife rather than the greatest queen on earth.
PILGRIM: I assure you that Drusilla is alive in person as long as she lives in your heart, and that she's wandering wretchedly through the world, thinking she's been abandoned by you.
LUCREZIO: Alas, what a strange thing you're saying! Please, don't raise my hopes with these dreams only to make me feel even worse when they turn out to be in vain.
PILGRIM: These are no dreams. I tell you that Drusilla lives provided that she can be yours, and to show you it's true I'll give you this bracelet on her behalf. Keep it until you're completely sure about her.
LUCREZIO: What am I hearing?
PILGRIM: Take it.
LUCREZIO: My God, this is the bracelet I placed around her arm when I left. I recognise it.

(At this point the Pilgrim takes off her cloak and hood).[127]

PILGRIM: Do you recognize me?
LUCREZIO: And are you really Drusilla? Drusilla, once dead and now risen from the dead? How can this be?
PILGRIM: Don't be afraid, my Lucrezio. I'm your Drusilla and I'm alive. I'm not dead, I never died. Neither did your friend lie

to you, since I was believed dead for many hours because of a serious accident, of which I'll tell you later on. I had even been placed on a bier where he saw me.

LUCREZIO: Oh Drusilla! Now I recognize you. My sweet Drusilla, my divine Drusilla, so you weren't dead?

PILGRIM: I was dead because I was deprived of you, who are my life. And now I am born once again for, having recovered you, I have recovered my soul.

LUCREZIO: Drusilla, my only love! I wept and sighed so much for you! Who brought you here?

PILGRIM: Desperation and love.

LUCREZIO: I can't stop hugging you. What did you set out to do? What did I do? How was this error possible?

PILGRIM: This is not the place for kissing or for telling such a long story. Let's go to the boarding house where Ricciardo is; he was with my uncle during our times in Seville. I know he's waiting for me and I want him to share in our joy.

LUCREZIO: Well,well! Is that Ricciardo?

PILGRIM: Yes, that's him. Also Tommasa is still in my service.

LUCREZIO: And is Tommasa, the faithful confidante of our thoughts, still with you? I'm so happy that she's here! Let's go and meet them; we'll take them all home.

PILGRIM: Yes, let's go! Now I've found that joy I told you about this morning, which meant so much to me and which I longed for so deeply.

LUCREZIO: I remember! I felt, when I looked at you, a kind of shiver which has lasted until now. It was because I thought I could see in your face some resemblance to Drusilla. But how could you find the courage to wait all this time before revealing yourself to me?

PILGRIM: Now you can understand my feelings. What made me do all this was the thought that you now belonged to another woman.

LUCREZIO: Before we go in, tell me, please, what you had come to tell me before.

PILGRIM: I had come to tell you that your Lepida was pregnant by the man who was employed in the house as a tutor and, after they found out that he was really a very noble gentleman, she was married to him.

LUCREZIO: Can it be true? I'm glad because, this way, I can get out of that marriage without arousing any disdain or rancour in the old man. He'll recognize the truth of my words, and see how rightly I complained and rebutted the accusation of being responsible for such an offence towards his daughter. How did they find this out?

PILGRIM: I'll tell you everything afterwards at more leisure. I was there. They were all set to send the gentleman to the galleys. But then they got everything straightened out, as you'll hear. It's a truly remarkable tale! Here, I won't keep it to myself. Messer Cassandro, having found out the truth, felt sorry he had disbelieved your words.

LUCREZIO: Let's go, then.

PILGRIM: Let's go in; I'm dying to cast off this pilgrim's dress since my pilgrimage is over. Now all my prayers and my wishes have been granted! [*Exeunt*]

NOTES

1 The occasion to which the author refers is the projected marriage between Christine of Lorraine and Ferdinando I, Grand Duke of Tuscany.
2 The author died in October, 1586 leaving behind his wife Silveria who was pregnant. She gave birth to a child on April 22, 1587; hence the reference to a 'posthumous' child.
3 It must be remembered that in Siena the calendar year was calculated *ab incarnatione* (March 25th); hence the date of the first dedicatory letter is March 4, 1588. By this stage the preparations for the wedding were truly under way. However, though Christine of Lorraine had been spoken for since the end of 1587, the wedding did not take place until May, 1589 (see Cerreta, *La Pellegrina*, 17 and the second dedicatory letter).
4 The motto means: out of sheer loyalty, as a result of innate dignity. At the end of the letter Scipione will thank Ferdinando for having adopted this motto and for having welcomed the presentation of the play. Scipione's fame for the composition of devices and *motti* is evidenced by his *La prima parte delle Imprese* (Venice, 1578) to which he later added a second and third part, and by *I rovesci delle medaglie* (Siena, 1599).
5 The original *orinali* is a reference to the urine test. Giglietta fears that the test might reveal that Lepida is pregnant. The test was a source of laughter in more than one sixteenth-century comedy; compare the scene in *La Mandragola* (Act II, sc. vi). Giglietta's speech, as with the very first repartee, is intentionally ambiguous; she is pretending to talk about Lepida's feigned madness while, in reality, she is worrying about the girl's pregnancy.
6 Doctors used to ride on mules to visit their patients.
7 According to Hippocratic medicine there are four fundamental biological humours which govern our character and disposition: blood, phlegm, yellow bile and black bile. Hence one could respectively be cheerful, phlegmatic, irascible or melancholic (see Cerreta, *op. cit.*, 76, note 4).
8 A prayer very common in the Middle Ages. It was usually recited by those who were about to set off on a voyage; see M.P. Giardini, *Tradizioni popolari nel "Decameron"* (Florence, 1965, 3). It was also a prayer recited to keep away various types of fever: the fever which comes on alternate days, *terzana*, and that which recurs every three days, peaking on the fourth, *quartana*. Here Giglietta claims that she recites it to undo the spell cast on Lepida. As for the other two prayers, the original *qui habitet* must be a popular corruption of *qui habitat in adjutorio Altissimi*, the first verse of psalm 90, one of the prayers recited by priests in exorcising devils; while the original *salvia regina* is a popular corruption of *salve regina* (see Cerreta, *op. cit.*, 77, note 7).
9 The original reads *Tenera come una brina*, literally *tender as frost*; this could be an ironic remark.

10 Rutilio is Lepida's brother; he is not mentioned in the *Dramatis personae* because he never appears on stage.
11 The original *parole studiate per lettera* once meant 'words studied in Latin'; here the more generic meaning is: words worthy of a scholar (see Borsellino, *La Pellegrina*, 439, note 26).
12 Amadìs de Gaula and Don Florisel de Niquela are two lucky heroes of Spanish chivalric poems; the former was immortalised in a poem by Garci Rodriguez de Montalvo. The subject matter of these Spanish poems of chivalry inspired Bernardo Tasso to write *Amadigi* and *Floridante* (see Borsellino, *op. cit.*, 440, note 2). Bargagli had already mentioned the characters in his *Dialogo* ed. cit., I, 246, 257, 269; II, 400, etc.
13 A reference to B. Castiglione's *Il Cortigiano* (III,70): it's the type of humanistic-pedantic language, made up of Latin expressions mixed with the vernacular, used in the *Hypnerotomachia Poliphili* attributed to Francesco Colonna (c.1499). Terenzio will resort to this type of language in various other passages in the play (see Borsellino, *op. cit.*, 441, note 7).
14 Jupiter, according to classical mythology, transformed himself into a bull to kidnap Europa and into a swan to seduce Leda.
15 The Lanfranchi are an old Pisan family.
16 The Italian *difetto* and *accidente* refer to Lepida's feigned madness.
17 Ponte di Mezzo in Pisa is the area where the play takes place.
18 The original *[libro] doppio*, a register book in which merchants wrote their debits and credits, lends itself to Cassandro's *ti vorrò a doppio bastone*, I'll give you twice as great a thrashing (see Borsellino, *op. cit.*, 451, note 2).
19 Giglietta's *scoppiati* from *coppia*, coupled, is taken by Cassandro in its other meaning, to burst, and emphasised by *crepati*, to die.
20 The inversion of terms is intended as a joke.
21 Cavicchia misunderstands *cappotto*, overcoat, for *cappe otto*, eight cloaks.
22 In the Renaissance Neapolitan silk was much prized; see P. Laven, *Renaissance Italy, 1464–1534* (London, 1966), 41–42.
23 Federigo's servant states that Germans usually court women to marry them, whereas Italians court women to make them their mistresses.
24 The original reads *pecora*, sheep, the animal which in the Renaissance was synonymous with stupidity.
25 The original reads *Salve, frater alter.*
26 The original reads *Domus versus.*
27 The original reads *puellulo.*
28 The university of Pisa.
29 The original reads *Intempestive.*
30 The original reads *diliculo.*
31 The name of an ancient family from Pisa.
32 The original reads *gratia tentandi.*

33 The original reads *verae nuptiae*.
34 The original reads *nihil ad te*.
35 The original reads *Satis est*.
36 The original reads *pro nunc*.
37 The original reads *natura paucis contenta est*.
38 The original, *omnis sapiens dives*, could be derived from the following Ciceronian expression *Sapientem locupletat ipsa Natura* (De Finibus, II,28,90), knowledge makes a man rich (see Cerreta, *op. cit.*, 100, note 31).
39 The original reads *optimo maximo*.
40 The original reads *pecunia*.
41 The original reads *Omnis labor optat praemium*.
42 The original reads *dignus est operaius mercede sua* which, according to Cerreta (*op. cit.*, 100, note 31), is taken from Luke, 10.7.
43 The original reads *valete*.
44 The original reads *[loqui] Latine, latine; ciceroniane, ciceroniane*. Messer Terenzio is wittily debunking the followers of Petrarch and the supporters of vulgar Italian; he contrasts them with those who strictly adhere to the *discipline liberali* which prepared students for the learning of philosophical and theological treatises in Mediaeval schools. The liberal studies consisted of the *Trivium* (grammar, rhetoric, dialectics) and the *Quadrivium* (arithmetic, geometry, music, astronomy).
45 The original reads *indignum facinus*.
46 It is impossible to render into English the change of one consonant which transforms *morte*, death as it was first (*ab initio*) called, into *corte*, court.
47 The analogy with *corte*, court is kept up in the original by the use of *corte*, short.
48 As above there is a play on the other meaning of *corte*, scanty, poor, of no significance.
49 One of the princes belonging to the royal family. After the fifteenth century, the members of this family, with the exclusion of the ruler, gained the right to bear the title of Archduke (see Cerreta, *op. cit.*, 101, note 36).
50 A reference to Cosimo I de' Medici who ruled Tuscany when the play was written (see Cerreta, *op. cit.*, 101, note 17); Borsellino (*op. cit.*, 457, note 19) believes that it refers to Ferdinando (see introduction).
51 According to popular belief, Cain had been condemned to carry a bundle of thorns and was to be identified with the spots on the moon; see Dante, *Inferno*, XX,126 and *Paradiso*, II,51 (see Cerreta, *op. cit.*, 102, note 38).
52 The inhabitants of Pisa had the nickname of *volpi*, foxes, in the sense of cheats (see Dante, *Purgatorio*, XIV,53).
53 Also known as Viridiana or Veridiana; she belonged to the third order of the Franciscan nuns and died around 1222 (see Cerreta, *op. cit.*, 113, note

44). Giglietta's reference to this saint is an ironic one since the name Monna Verdiana, after the characterisation made by Boccaccio in the *Decameron* (V,10), came to be used in sixteenth-century Italian theatre (see G.M. Cecchi's *L'Assiuolo*, Act I, sc. ii) as a stock character, that of the old procuress. Giglietta is obviously making reference to her role in the plot as a go-between.

54 All the above expressions have sexual connotations and are reminiscent of the situation experienced by Agnoletta in A. Piccolomini's *L'Amor costante* (Act II, sc. x) (see Borsellino, *op. cit.*, 467, note 1).

55 This expression also lends itself to an obscene *double entendre*.

56 The original reads *È un peccato che tu non sii un di questi gran maestri, poichè ti lasci vedere così a punti di luna*. The *punti di luna* are the points, intervals between one new moon and another, while the *gran maestri* are the leaders or, more commonly, the important persons in a community (see Aretino, *Ragionamenti*, Day III, part II). Though not self-evident, the sense of Violante's ironic dig is the following: you show up so rarely that one would think that you are an important person, absorbed in great occupations; it's a pity that you are not (such an important person) (see Borsellino, *op. cit.*, 468, note 5).

57 Violante thinks that Carletto's master wants her to act as a go-between, as a Madonna Verdiana; hence her reaction. The procuress was usually old, bigoted and had been a whore in her younger days.

58 Here, as in other cases, the text has *forestieri*. But they are foreigners only in so far as they come from outside the city and not necessarily from abroad.

59 The original *non è terreno da porci vigna* renders more colourfully and materialistically the fact that one cannot rely on this pilgrim to obtain anything just as one cannot harvest grapes from an unsuitable terrain.

60 Carletto's last two expressions lend themselves to a sexual *double entendre*.

61 The original reads *Here salve*.

62 The original reads *quomodo res se habeant*.

63 The original reads *auxilio*.

64 The proverb, not completed in the text by Messer Terenzio, is derived from Horace, *Carmina* (II,10): *Sperat infestis, metuit secundis/ [Alteram sortem bene praeparatum/ pectus]* (see Borsellino, *op. cit.*, 471, note 4): the well prepared spirit hopes in times of adversity and fears in times of prosperity.

65 As already seen (see note 7), according to Hippocrates, this is one of the four humours and is the direct opposite to the sanguine disposition (happy and self-assured) which is considered the best to possess.

66 The original reads *Sapienter quidem*.

67 The words of Micione, the indulgent old bachelor in Terence's *Adelphoe*

(Act I, sc. i, v.57), are: *Pudore et liberalitate liberos/ [retinere satius esse credo quam metu]*. Messer Terenzio quotes only the first half; the quotation means: it is always best to try and control our children by care and benevolence rather than by fear (see Cerreta, *op. cit.*, 118, note 54).
68 The original reads *quotidie*.
69 The original reads *Forsitan*.
70 The original reads *muliercula venefica*.
71 Messer Terenzio's words, ironic in the context, are given in Latin, *Adhuc virum non cognoscit*, perhaps to disguise his embarrassment.
72 The original reads *Cave, cave*.
73 The original reads *Tanto magis*.
74 The original reads *ut luceant coram hominibus*.
75 The original reads *precipue*.
76 Aesculapius was the god of medicine in Greek mythology and one of the popular subjects of ancient art, usually depicted with a snake (symbol of rejuvenescence).
77 The original reads *experimentum fallax*.
78 The original reads *Praeterea*.
79 The original reads *Bonis avibus*.
80 One of the five fundamental elements of nature: Aristotle uses the name to mean 'ether,' believing that it was the substance of which the celestial world was composed. Here it stands to indicate the 'etheral' quality of Targhetta who is never to be found. According to Borsellino (op. cit., 474, note 1) it is the mysterious substance sought by alchemists to make the elixir of life.
81 This passage in which Targhetta exposes the practices of the priests is reminiscent of the one we find in the *Decameron* (III,7).
82 The original reads *Balia [Giglietta]*; for reasons of continuity I have kept the Christian name.
83 In the text the language lends itself to a comic paradox since the adjective *savia*, wise, is in antithesis to *matta*, crazy.
84 As in the previous note we have another example of comic paradox where *spropositi*, blunders, is antithetically opposed to *a proposito*, appropriate.
85 The original reads *quando si ballava co' guanti e col fazzoletto*, when people danced with gloves and handkerchiefs, an expression which might derive, according to Borsellino, from the following passage of the prologue to Aretino's *Il Marescalco:* "et al mio tempo ballai . . . con una Signora, però col fazzoletto, perchè allora non si poteva toccare la mano a le donne ballando" (and in my days I danced . . . with a lady, with the handkerchief though, since at that time one couldn't touch a woman's hand while dancing) (see Borsellino, *op. cit.*, 479, note 5).
86 The original reads *costui*, this man. Obviously Lepida is pointing in the direction of her father.

87 Lepida is referring to the outcome of the monk's visit.
88 The original *buona limosina* is used in the same ironic sense by Aretino in his *Ragionamenti*, Day II, part II (see Borsellino, *op. cit.*, 486, note 3).
89 The original *che tu possa scoppiare!*, may you burst, is more immediate.
90 The original has a play on words between *astuccio*, vanity-case, and *astuto*, astute, crafty.
91 The original popular expression is *mio mio come il nibbio* derived from imitating the sound made by the *nibbio*, kite, which seems to be *mio mio*.
92 The original *andare alla ragione* means to appeal to a court.
93 The original has a play on words: *io sarò la balia e tu sarai la baia* where *baia*, fooled, is set against *balia*, nurse.
94 The original *s'io ho guasto il tabarro mi guastarebbeno il giubbone ancora* indicates the greater trouble that Targhetta would get into if he took the people to court. He talks about the possibility of greater damage (*guasto*) by referring to two pieces of clothing: the *tabarro* is a cloak while the *giubbone* is a type of light jacket but also a word used in the idiomatic sentence, *spolverare il giubbone*, to beat someone up; Targhetta is, therefore, afraid of greater physical harm if he complains about the armed people invented in the story to Carletto.
95 The original *che vogli pigliarti gli impacci del Rosso* is a Tuscan proverb used by G.M. Cecchi in his *L'Assiuolo* and is explained in his collection of *Proverbi Toscani;* both works are to be found in volume VIII of *Biblioteca Rara* edited by G. Daelli (Milan, 1863) where we find Cecchi's explanation of the proverb: Rosso was a thief being led to the gallows on a cart and he complained about the disgraceful state of the road which jolted him about; hence the proverb denoting someone who worries about unnecessary matters (72, note 51).
96 This is said ironically.
97 There is a series of plays on words based on the name Carletto: *carlona*, happy-go-lucky, *carletta*, a diminutive of *Carla* with a contextual meaning opposite to *carlona*, *carlin*, a Neapolitan coin of the time.
98 The original is more effective since there is only a change of one letter between *lettere*, studies, and *lettiere*, beds.
99 An exaggeration of Messer Federigo's inability to appreciate good food and good wine. These expressions are meant to emphasise the poor quality of the food.
100 Cavicchia is referring to the lack of hygiene which is indicated by the crust—hence the reference to *corazza*, armour—on the kitchenware.
101 The original *Guarda qui se cencio mi dice straccio* literally means: who's ever heard of a rag (*cencio*) throwing accusations at a cloth (*straccio*).
102 Cavicchia is saying that the wine, having been watered down, has been cleansed of its sins just as a baby is when it is christened.

THE FEMALE PILGRIM 153

103 Violante plays on the etymology of *Cavicchia*, a type of wooden nail, and its connotative connection with the male sexual organ.
104 Cavicchia plays on the word *viola* with reference to both Violante and the female genitalia.
105 A punishment reserved for prostitutes and women accused of petty crimes: their skirts were cut off at the waist and they were whipped on their bare buttocks.
106 Targhetta is portrayed as the classical *currens servus*, running servant, who arrives breathless, delays the communication of news which the master is anxious to hear, and expects a tip for his troubles (see Cerreta, *op. cit.*, 168, note 96).
107 The confusion arising from the name is further exploited in sc. iii and is finally cleared up in Act V, sc. iv.
108 This is a comic reference to Astolfo's trip to the moon to regain Orlando's wits in Ariosto's *Orlando Furioso* (see Cerreta, *op. cit.*, p.172, note 97 and Borsellino, *op. cit.*, 519, note 2).
109 Messer Federigo hides the real intention which led him to the courtyard (see Act III, sc. v).
110 Giglietta creates a *double entendre* with reference to the climax (*in sul buono*) of the lovers' passionate encounter and that of Lepida's actions while feigning madness, *quel suo umore le fa far certi atti*.
111 The original *murate*, walled in, refers to those nuns who observe an even stricter enclosure than the *racchiuse*, enclosed nuns.
112 The *commessario* was the representative of the Florentine government at the time Pisa was subject to Florentine rule.
113 The prisoners, in those days, were condemned to row in galleys; hence the reference to *galera*, jail, at the end of the Officer's speech.
114 A reference to Cosimo I de' Medici on whom the title of Grand Duke was officially conferred in 1569 (see also Act IV, sc. vi).
115 According to Borsellino (*op.cit.*, 533, note 6) university students, especially the foreign ones, enjoyed special privileges under the chancellor's jurisdiction, as if they belonged to regular corporations.
116 A very ancient Florentine family whose palace is still standing in Piazza Santo Spirito.
117 In those days it was called Flanders (*Fiandra*).
118 There is a play on words between the meaning of *dieta*, Diet, and *dieta*, food diet.
119 The wisdom of this biblical king has become proverbial.
120 The names of wines of good quality.
121 A very ordinary wine as the name suggests: *posticcio*, false, artificial; also the wine grown in flat country (*di piano*) is considered of inferior quality.
122 They are examples of men who betrayed their beloved: in Greek mythol-

ogy Theseus abandoned Ariadne on the island of Naxos after having obtained her help to kill the Minotaur and in the *Orlando Furioso* (canto X) Bireno deceives Olimpia.

123 Messer Federigo plays on the double meaning of *banco*, the place on a galley where Messer Terenzio will be chained, and *banco*, a writing desk.

124 These were made unlawful by the decree *de clandestinis matrimoniis* promulgated by the Tridentine Council on August 7, 1563; this decree was effective from May 1, 1564 (see Cerreta, *op. cit.*, 193, note 117).

125 The name, of Austrian origin, is found in the Galeotto Malatesti story (Pecorone, VII, 2); it also appeared in *Paradiso*, XVI, 89 as the name of the oldest Florentine family remembered by Cacciaguida (see Cerreta, *op. cit.*, 193, note 119).

126 It can either be Innsbruck or Bruck (see Cerreta, *op. cit.*, 195, note 122 and Borsellino, *op. cit.*, 541, note 20).

127 The original *abito* should be interpreted as being a cloak since Drusilla goes into the house to get rid of her pilgrim disguise only after the last exchange.